The Great Soviet Awakening

The True Story
the West
Was Never Told

by Tom Kraeuter

© 2012 Training Resources, Inc.
65 Shepherds Way
Hillsboro, MO 63050
(636) 789-4522
www.training-resources.org

ISBN   978-1-932096-98-9

Cover: Artist's rendering of Oleviste Church, Tallinn, Estonia. Original cover art by Hanna & Erkki Tamsalu, via www.Shutterstock.com. Altered and adapted by Tom Kraeuter.

Dedication

I humbly dedicate this book to Rein Uuemõis. Although we've only met in person a couple of times, I have encountered your legacy through numerous people that I interviewed from multiple countries. Thank you for allowing the Lord to work in and through your life in tremendous ways. Thank you, also, for giving me your blessing to write this story. If my life could have a small fraction of the impact yours has made, I would consider myself blessed beyond measure.

Thanks to:

- Ülo Niinemägi for tireless work in setting up interviews, translating, chauffeuring me around Estonia, accomodating last minute changes, and so much more.

- Amy Kraeuter for video recording most of the interviews.

- Kevin and Debbie Campbell for investing in and encouragment for this project right from the start.

- Jennifer Brody, Diane Lopez, Fran Moore, and Conie Wood for editing and proofreading at various stages along the way.

- Katrin Kikerpill and Nele Otto for excellent translation and transcription work, without which, I would not have had access to much source material for this book.

- John & Janet Klippel and Scott & Amy Woodruff for investing in the publishing of this book.

- My wonderful wife and family for allowing me the time to write and for offering suggestions on the manuscript.

Contents

Prologue

Just three brief decades ago, something startling happened in the Kingdom of God here on earth. I would dare to suggest that it was an occurrence of biblically-epic proportions. When I first heard an extremely condensed version of the story, I was shocked. It was an overwhelming tale of God's grace made tangible in amazing ways.

I have been a Christian for more than thirty-five years. I've been in full-time ministry for twenty-five years, ministering in churches all across North America and even other parts of the world. However, I had never heard so much as an inkling of this story before. The truth is that the vast majority of Christians know nothing about it, but it is a faith-strengthening story from which we can learn much.

The opening chapter is entirely true, except for Matti, a fictional character. Matti is only there to fit the pieces together. The specific details have all come from eyewitnesses of the actual account. †

Chapter 1

A Snapshot

According to the calendar, spring officially began four days ago, but winter was clearly not ready to loosen its grip. Large snowflakes floated gently downward and seemed to increase in size as they passed the bluish light of the lone streetlamp. It was an older, mostly residential neighborhood in a large city, and an elderly woman with an oversized bag trudged along the sidewalk, obviously being very cautious not to slip on the newly fallen snow.

Fortunately, this late-March snowfall didn't show signs of any real accumulation, and Matti was glad as he tried to hurry along opposite the old woman. He didn't want to be slowed down any more than he was already. He had left his house later than he intended, and that was compounded by his sprained ankle that hindered his movement as he hobbled along the sidewalk. He was already late, and he felt as though he was getting later by the moment.

For just a brief instant Matti's thoughts about his tardiness were set aside. Instead, his attention was drawn to the nearly empty street. It seemed odd to him that this area was almost barren, especially since he knew that just two streets away there would be a bustle of activity.

He did his best to hurry along on his swollen ankle. When he finally turned the corner, sure enough, he could see dozens of people pouring through the doors of the old church building. He knew that hundreds more were already gathered inside.

Just a short distance down the street, Matti heard a group of people laughing. As he turned and glanced toward them, he nearly stumbled on the one worn stone step that led to the door of the church. He caught himself before falling, but it made him remember. Just a few months earlier Matti had visited the old church for the first time, and he had tripped on the same step then. Matti had smiled when it happened originally. This time, though, he winced in pain as he steadied himself on his impaired ankle.

As he walked into the crowded foyer, his eyes quickly adjusted to the light. He made his way to the sanctuary door on the right, trying to skirt around a small group of people who were talking in a language he didn't understand. This door to the right was the one he had used on his first visit, and he had continued that same pattern each time since.

Through the open door, Matti saw hundreds of people. On his last visit, he had speculated that there were well over a thousand in attendance, but he didn't actually take the time to count. The worn wooden benches were filled to overflowing, and people stood — some even sat — in the aisleways all around the perimeter. With so many people packed in like sardines, and given the size of the auditorium, surely there must be more than a thousand, he thought. Matti had been told that these three-times-a-month meetings had begun with only youth. Now, a few years later, there were people — and lots of them — of all ages, infants to the very elderly.

Glancing upward, Matti wondered again — for the umpteenth time perhaps? — how high the ceiling really was in this ancient cathedral. It never ceased to amaze him how the place could have been built without the aid of modern machinery. It was a huge edifice, and he had often wondered what it must have looked like when it was new.

Matti was trying to decide where he might sit — he knew he should have left home sooner — when he heard someone call his name. He turned and saw a group of his friends waving to him. He had only recently met most of them, but they had become friends quickly because of their shared experiences at the church meetings. Most people in their society didn't look too kindly on "church people," so they had a tendency to hang together.

Matti quickly made his way through the crowd to where his friends were sitting. They greeted him enthusiastically, glad he had made it.

"Did you hear the news?" asked one of the girls excitedly. "Joanna became a Christian yesterday."

"*Joanna?!*" responded Matti, obviously skeptical. Joanna was one of their classmates who was very vocal about her opposition to the Christian faith. "Are you sure?"

"Yes. She told me herself last night. She came to the meeting two weeks ago just to get more information to challenge us with. But apparently she was convicted by what she heard. Yesterday she received the Lord's forgiveness." The young lady looked around the sanctuary. "She should be here somewhere."

Matti shook his head, once again astonished by God's amazing grace. *Joanna, of all people*, he thought.

Just then a man at the front of the church began talking. "We welcome all of you here tonight. We want to especially welcome those who have come from far away. We are very glad you have joined us." The man smiled. He looked out over the congregation as the crowd began to settle in for the service. "We believe that God's Word should be preeminent, so we will begin by reading Scripture." He paused as he opened his Bible. "I will be read-

opposed to Matti's newfound faith. The new life he began that night was a decisive turning point for him. He could remember practically every detail of that night like it had just happened moments before. It was actually months ago now.

The song finished and the choir and band returned to their seats in the front. A man came to the center of the platform. He was not a tall man, perhaps about forty or so. He looked to the front pew and motioned for a woman to come forward. She slowly walked to the front, but she was obviously very nervous. The man said, "This woman has come from a long distance away to tell about what God has done in her life."

The woman timidly began to share. "I have come to testify of what God has done for me through your prayers." She smiled, trying to appear less nervous than she was. "I am a nurse. I came here to one of the services like this four months ago. I had neck cancer. It had spread into my throat, and it was so bad that my mouth was bleeding constantly. That's when I came here... like I said, four months ago." She looked at the man and then back at the crowd. "The brothers here prayed for me." The woman stopped, clearly on the verge of tears. She struggled to hold her emotions in check, and it took only a few seconds for her to regain her composure. Then she continued, "I thank God, because from that day a change occurred. Cancer cells started to disappear, and, as you can see, I am completely well." She opened her mouth wide and moved her head back and forth, displaying the inside of her mouth. "Thanks to Jesus, through His blood, I have recovered." The listeners applauded — some shouted praise to God.

The man smiled broadly and then gently led the woman back to her seat. He slowly returned to the platform with his head bowed, perhaps contemplating what to say next. He looked up and said, "Let me read you another testimony we just received in the mail." He pulled a piece of paper from his shirt pocket. "It says, 'I came to one of the special services two weeks ago. I was a cripple, and I had to use crutches to walk. At the service, I was prayed for, and God healed me. Now I am well and work as a bricklayer.'" The reader paused. "A formerly crippled man who is now a bricklayer." The man shook his head in astonishment. "This is just one of the many letters we receive regularly." People again clapped enthusiastically.

The man stood quietly for a moment at the front center of the platform. He was holding only a Bible, and he looked out at the throng of people. "Now let me talk with you for a few moments." He smiled a broad, infectious smile, but then took on a more sober countenance as he began to speak. "In Isaiah 59:12, the Bible says, 'For our transgressions are multiplied before you, and our sins testify against us; for our transgressions are with us, and we know our iniquities...'" He paused, just long enough to let those words sink in. "I think this passage describes our situation — yours and mine — perfectly." He stopped and then started in again.

"Do you see this yellow shirt I'm wearing?" he asked.

"Now keep in mind, I'm not a pastor. I'm an engineer. I work in a regular job, just like most of you. Anyway, I wore this same shirt a few days ago." He paused and smiled. "Don't worry. It's been washed since then." He chuckled a bit. "When I put it on that morning it was clean. In fact, it was really clean, but I noticed when I got home that evening that it was no longer clean." He looked around at the crowd of people. "Now remember, I don't work in a factory. My job is in an office. And it's a neat and well-kept office. There is not a lot of dirt and grime at my desk or even the other desks that are near mine. Overall, we're a pretty clean group of people."

"But I noticed when I got home that my clean yellow shirt was no longer so clean. There was a smudge over here," he pointed to his right shoulder, "that I think I must have gotten from the tram on the way home. And there was a small spot right down here," he pointed down near his stomach, "that was probably from lunch." He grinned. "The shirt wasn't covered with mud or grease. In fact, some people might not have even noticed the couple of spots. But I knew it needed to be laundered."

Matti loved the fact that the messages during these meetings were simple and easy to understand. He didn't need to strain to try to comprehend what was being said. He could always relate to it.

"It wasn't some major spot that made the shirt un-clean. There were no huge stains. No, there were just a couple of little things." The man paused briefly before continuing his train of thought. "Some of you here tonight think that your little sins don't really make that much difference — to you or to God or to anyone else. After all, they're only little sins. Not worth even bothering about. They're insignificant things that aren't really all that important, right?" He waited briefly for an acknowledgement from the crowd. "But from God's perspective, those very things make you unacceptable to Him. A holy God cannot co-exist with — or even tolerate — your 'little' sins."

"The Bible says that 'the wages of sin is death.' That's an odd phrase to our minds: 'The wages of sin.' What exactly is 'the wages of sin'? Think about it this way. Wages are what you earn for doing a job. So what does sin 'earn'? According to the Bible, it earns death. That's what you get paid for your sins. Death. And not just death from this life. Eternal death. Ongoing permanent separation from God. Hell." The boy next to Matti squirmed a bit in his seat, obviously uncomfortable with this idea. "And it doesn't have to be what we might consider big sins, either. Even little ones earn the same wages. A small lie. A tiny evil thought. Taking something little that doesn't belong to you." The man stopped again for just a moment.

"Let me tell you a story. At the end of World War II, German Field Marshal Hermann Göring was captured. In Nazi Germany, he was second in command only to Hitler himself. At the Nuremberg Trials, Göring was tried and convicted of war crimes and crimes against humanity. His sentence stated that he was to die by hanging. Considering the horrendous weight of his crimes, Göring was going to get what he deserved. His brutal deeds would receive a brutal penalty. But Göring did not want to die at the hands of the Allies. He would much rather have committed suicide than to give them the satisfaction of ending his life. Maybe the Allies knew this. I'm not certain. In any event, though, they kept him under constant surveillance. They were definitely not going to make suicide easy for him, that's for certain."

"I've been told that the night before he was to be hanged, Göring's wife, Emmy, visited him. They had not seen one another for some time, and they were not allowed much contact. During her visit, though, she was permitted to give her husband a kiss, one small touch of their lips together. It was seemingly a simple gesture of their years of marriage. But unknown to the guards, Emmy held a tiny capsule between her teeth. The capsule was filled with cyanide. When they kissed, she carefully slipped it between Göring's lips. He knew what she was doing and readily accepted the capsule. Once he had it in his mouth, he swallowed it and the deed was done. After Emmy left, the guards found Göring dead in his cell." The preacher looked out at the spellbound listeners. They collectively waited for his next words.

"Keep in mind that it wasn't a large capsule that killed him. It didn't take a lot of poison to snuff out his life. Of course, a lot of poison would have done the job — and done it very effectively — but that wasn't necessary. It was just a very small amount. Only a tiny capsule. That's all it took. It was enough. Just that little bit." Another thoughtful delay, and he continued. "Your sins don't need to be huge. A little lustful thought. A small greedy inclination. Even such seemingly minor things separate you from a God Who is pure and perfect."

"Some of you here tonight take things home with you from your job, perhaps a bundle of paper or some tools or something else. Those things don't actually belong to you, but, well, it's not a big deal. It's not so bad. After all, everyone else is doing it, so why not, right?" The speaker stopped and gazed out at the congregation. "Right?" He paused again for emphasis, and a few heads nodded slightly. "But let's be really candid for a moment. What you're doing is called 'stealing' and it's a sin."

"The truth is that God is holy, and we are unholy. Our sins separate us from Him. The Bible tells us that *all* have sinned and fall short of the glory of God. All of us. There isn't one of us who has not sinned. Everyone in this room has fallen short." He let those words sink in for a moment. "In the New Testament, the word that is most commonly translated into our language as 'sin' literally means 'to miss the mark.' Think about it this way. If you shoot an arrow at a target, and you miss the target, it makes precious little difference whether you missed it by just a tiny bit or by a lot; you still missed it. Whether your sins are big or small, you have still missed God's standard."

Just then a baby cried on the other side of the room from Matti. The man intentionally spoke louder to be sure he was heard. "And you can't somehow make yourself better in God's sight. The Apostle Paul — who wrote much of the New Testament — was one of the most righteous people of his day. But he said that all his virtuousness, all his hard-earned credentials, all his goodness, were nothing compared with knowing Christ. You see, when Jesus died on the cross, He took our sins — mine, yours, everybody's — and paid for them. That's why Paul treasured knowing Christ so highly. It is the only way we can become holy in God's sight. Our works will never be enough. Never. But through Jesus' death and resurrection, you and I have been reconciled to the Lord, accepted by Him. Our sins have been forgiven, and we can now be in right relationship with God Almighty."

"Tonight, some of you feel like you're drowning and God is throwing you a life-preserver: a relationship with Himself through Jesus."

"It says in the Bible that one day Jesus met a woman at a well. It is an interesting story, and maybe sometime we'll look at the whole thing. But for now, I want to zero in on one aspect. Jesus said He was thirsty and asked her for a drink. She was surprised by His request, but He followed up by saying, 'If you knew the gift of God, and who it is that is saying to you, "Give me a drink," you would have asked him, and he would have given you living water.'"[2] Matti tried to picture the scene in his mind.

"Clearly the woman didn't understand," said the preacher. "After all, how could the guy who had just asked her for a drink now be offering *her* one? It just didn't make sense. But Jesus went on to say that if someone drank the water she drew from the well, that person would become thirsty again. 'But whoever drinks of the water that I will give him will never be thirsty again. The water that I will give him will become in him a spring of water welling up to eternal life.'"[3] The man paused long enough for the people to grasp the words, then continued. "Jesus wasn't talking about water like you get from a faucet or a stream or a well. That kind of water will only satisfy for a short time. Jesus was talking about something far better, far more satisfying."

"Imagine it like this. You're in a desert. It's a vast desert that goes on and on. You're already three days' journey into the desert, and you know it's at least that far to the other side. And you just ran out of water. But then something amazing happens. Jesus Himself comes to you. He is suddenly standing in front of you. If that was you — and you were pretty sure you were dying of thirst — and Jesus suddenly appeared out of nowhere, what would you ask Him for?" Again he stopped, allowing the hearers to imagine the scenario. "A glass of water? A bucket of water? You could ask for those... and He could give them. That would be easy for Jesus. But He's offering you so much more. He doesn't want to give you just a gulp of water. He wants to give you Himself. And when you have Him, you'll get a whole ocean of water... and everything else you need, also."

"Tonight, some of you here are thirsty, with a thirst that no earthly water can quench. You know there's more to life than just what you've experienced so far. When you're in right relationship with the Creator — I mean *right* relationship, not the sin-distanced relationship that we so often experience — then all of life changes. I'm not saying you're always going to be happy. Jesus does not stop all the bad things from happening in your life. But even when you experience pain and sorrow, He will bring you more true peace and joy than you've ever known before. It all begins, though, by renouncing your sins — the big ones and the little ones — and receiving His forgiveness."

"So here's my question to you: Are you ready tonight to receive that forgiveness? Are you ready to admit that you are a sinful person, that your sin separates you from God, and that you need His forgiveness through Jesus Christ? If so, I want you to raise your hand." Matti glanced about and saw dozens of hands raised. "Now that you've done that, I want to invite you — but only if you're serious — to come forward. Please realize that there is nothing magical about coming up here to the front of the church. You can receive Christ's forgiveness right there in the pew, or even in the quietness of your own home. The actual location isn't the issue. But there *is* something about making a public declaration of your faith that solidifies it more in your heart and mind. So I'm asking if you really want to receive God's forgiveness, and want to know Him in a new and even a personal way, would you make your way up here to the front and allow the members of the choir to pray for you?"

People all across the sanctuary rose from their seats to walk forward. By the time it was done, more than fifty people had gathered around the altar area. Many were young people, but there were some older ones, too. Matti knew this was pretty normal. The once-a-month Sunday evening service was usually a bit lighter in numbers, but the two Saturday night services each month — like this one — were always packed, and the response to the altar invitation was usually about this size or larger.

As the people made their way to the front, the choir members stood to go and pray with them. At the same time, another man asked those who would like prayers for healing to go quickly and quietly through the door to the right of the altar area.

Matti thought back to the night he responded to the altar call. There was something far greater than just the words that were said. Somehow he knew that God was offering him a fresh start, a brand new beginning. Matti knelt at the front between an older woman and another youth about his own age. One of the choir members, a man — perhaps in his mid-twenties — knelt on the other side of the altar rail and prayed with Matti.

Tonight, though, Matti stood and headed for the door off to the right side of the altar. The ankle he had sprained at school a few days ago may have seemed minor compared to some of the ailments of others, but Matti wanted it to be better. Injuring it was a stupid mistake, really. He was walking up the steps at school — okay, almost running up the steps might be a better way of saying it — hurrying to class. Just as he was about to make the right-angle turn there on the crowded stairway, one of his friends had called to him. As Matti turned his head, he somehow missed the next step. His ankle turned, and down he went. Hard. Then, to make matters worse, another student stepped right on the ankle and fell down on top of him. Matti barely made it to class on time, but he couldn't focus during the session. The pain was intense. His ankle began to swell, and he could barely walk. Now, four days later, the swelling had gone down, but only a little. It still hurt to walk, and an offer for healing sounded really good, so Matti made his way toward the door to the room they call Mary Chapel.

Since Matti was sitting on the right side of the church, he was one of the first twenty or thirty people into the room. It was a good thing, too, because by the time everyone had crowded in, the room was packed full. Standing-room only. Probably more than two-hundred people had crammed in there. As the last few stragglers made their way through the door, the man in the yellow shirt — the one who had been preaching — immediately invited people to make their way forward for healing. He asked them to form three lines. There would be people at the front of each line who would minister to those who wanted prayer.

Matti got into the middle line. He thought that it might afford him the best opportunity to see what happened in all three lines. He had, of course, heard the testimonies. Week after week people shared about healings, some that sounded almost unbelievable, but they apparently really happened. Matti was looking forward to seeing for himself.

At the front of the line to the left, he saw a very tall man. The man's height seemed exaggerated by the fact that his wife, standing next to him, was unusually short. The man stood, but only with the aid of crutches. When it was his turn, the yellow-shirted man stood with his hands on his hips, looked the tall man right in the eyes, and said to him, "Stand up and walk." Matti thought this a bit odd since the man was already standing. The man on crutches just looked at him for a moment. Then, Matti saw the man stand up straighter and even taller than he had been. Next he bent slightly from side to side, back and forth. He then dropped one crutch onto the floor. The man steadied himself with the remaining crutch to be sure he was able to stand. When he felt confident, he threw aside the other crutch. A huge smile crossed his face. With that smile, he jumped up and down and actually ran around in the small area that was available. He stopped and scooped up his wife and hugged her. Her hands covering her mouth, and the tears in her eyes, told the whole story: her husband had been instantly healed. After profusely shaking the hand of the yellow-shirted man and repeatedly thanking him, the tall man picked up his crutches and placed them in a corner near the front. Then he and his wife headed toward the door. He was obviously a happy — and healed — man.

Matti had trouble taking his eyes off the man as he headed out the door. He had never before witnessed — at least not firsthand — anything like this. It was a true miracle, and it had happened right there in front of his eyes.

Since there were still a couple of people in front of him in his own line, Matti looked to the front of the line to his right. A middle-aged man had just reached the front of that line. He was being led by a companion, and Matti heard the man say something about having developed glaucoma. "I can see things only as shadows. I can just barely see you now, and only as dark, featureless figures," said the man to the ones who were about to pray for him. "Even when I look at the full sun up in the sky, it appears like there is a thick mist over it."

"That's not too big an issue for God to take care of," said one of the brothers. "Let's pray."

Matti couldn't quite make out all the words they prayed, but the moment they said, "In the name of Jesus Christ, the risen Lord," something happened. The man looked around. He looked up and down, back and forth. His head jerked about as though he was trying to take in all the sights at once. Then he shouted, "I can see!" His eyesight apparently had been completely restored. The man turned and looked at the people behind him. He looked at each one very intently, as though he was seeing people for the first time. Well, it wasn't the very first time, but it was the first time in a long time.

Matti smiled at the thought of seeing yet another miracle and then shifted his weight as he began to move forward in his own line. As he did this, he suddenly noticed that his ankle didn't hurt anymore. He tried stretching the ankle from side to side, and up and down. No pain. Not even a little. He reached down and touched his ankle and... the swelling was gone. He smiled again. He realized he no longer needed to be prayed for. He had already been healed. He recalled a man a few weeks ago who had given a testimony about being healed while he was still waiting in line. *It happened again*, thought Matti. *This time to me!*

Matti decided he really didn't need to stay there in line. His ankle felt great. He turned and walked out the door, heading for home, praising God all the way.

Everything that Matti saw and experienced in this chapter really did happen. The message that was shared, the testimonies, the salvations, the healings — I did not make any of this up. In fact, if you keep reading, you'll realize that this chapter is only the very smallest tip of a really, really huge iceberg. Tens of thousands of people were impacted directly inside the walls of the church. Tens of thousands more — perhaps hundreds of thousands — were impacted as the revival spread. Hundreds of churches were started as a result. People were born-again and physically healed by nothing less than the power of God.

If such a thing happened in, say, St. Louis, Missouri, or Sacramento, California, we would think it was amazing. The truth, though, is that it really did occur in a city about the size of St. Louis or Sacramento, but it wasn't in the U.S. In fact, it happened in Tallinn, Estonia, part of the former Soviet Union. The Lord performed these miraculous signs, all while the Communists persecuted the believers and continued to deny that God even existed. As startling as all of those facts are, there is another part of the story that is, perhaps, even more amazing. The miracles, the preaching of the gospel, the salvations, all happened next door to the KGB Headquarters for the entire western Soviet Union. I don't mean that the headquarters was a little ways down the road. No, it was right next door. The Soviet secret police had a surveillance camera mounted on their building pointed at the front door of the church to keep an eye on what was happening there. Still, God moved in miraculous ways in spite of the authorities.

It's likely that you've never heard anything about this amazing revival that affected thousands and thousands of people all across the Soviet Union. If you haven't, keep reading. You may well be as startled as I was when I first encountered this story. Although I have a really active and vivid imagination, the true story is far more amazing than anything I could make up. †

Chapter 2

Beginnings

I'm not entirely certain which detail I found more shocking. It might have been the idea that almost no one in the West had ever heard the story before, or perhaps it was the fact that it all happened under the Soviet Communist regime. Whichever one it was, the six others who were with me — four of us from North America and three from Finland — sat transfixed as the nearly eighty-year-old pastor told us the story.

Tallinn, Estonia, has a tremendous Christian heritage. There is even a road there named Holy Spirit Street. Several ancient church buildings are scattered throughout the old city.

However, Tallinn also has a history of oppression:

> When the King of Denmark, Valdemar II, arrived in 1219, the ancient independence of Estonians was over until the 20th century. Having torn down the Estonian stronghold, Valdemar II proceeded to erect his own — the Danish Castle, or taani linnus, from which Tallinn takes its name. Within the following seven centuries Tallinn belonged to the Danes, Germans, Swedes and Russians....[1]

Except for a brief twenty-year period between the two World Wars, and now, since the fall of the Iron Curtain, Tallinn, Estonia, was under the control of other nations for nearly eight hundred years.

As a point of reference, Estonia is the northernmost of the three Baltic States, along with Lithuania and Latvia. It is east of Sweden and west of Russia. Tallinn, the capitol city, is a short two-hour ferry ride due south from Helsinki, Finland.

Oleviste Church — St. Olaf's in English — is a huge ancient cathedral believed to have been built in the 1100s. The enormous steeple is more than 400 feet tall. For seventy-six years (1549-1625), it was the tallest building in the world. Approaching by boat (from the Bay of Finland), it is the first object visible. For centuries, ships and boats have used that mammoth spire as a guide. The main ceiling of the sanctuary must be nearly a hundred feet high with majestic support arches holding it in place. By any standards, it is a magnificently preserved example of gothic architecture. More important than the physical building, though, is the spiritual history of the church.

I first ministered at Oleviste Church in May, 2009. The truth is, my being there was the result of a mistake. Well... at least from my human perspective it was an error. My plans for this trip to Finland and Estonia had changed. I had decided that it would be best for me to go only to Finland where I was to teach at a conference, and the others could take care of the ministry needs in Estonia. Somehow, though, my flights didn't get changed. Instead of leaving from Finland, I was scheduled to fly out of the airport in Tallinn on Monday morning. So, after ministering in a church in Helsinki on Saturday night, I took the ferry across the Bay of Finland — from Helsinki, Finland, to Tallinn, Estonia. I would be there in time to get a bit of rest and then preach for the first of three services at Oleviste Church on Sunday morning. I saw it as a mistake, but God's perception was considerably different than mine.

So, there I sat, after the third service that day, with others who had also just ministered at the same conference in Finland. We listened to the slow, occasionally halting English of our host, the former senior pastor, Rein Uuemõis — the man in the yellow shirt in the opening story — as he shared his amazing story. It was a brief glimpse of Oleviste's history.

In 1950, the Soviets were solidly in control of Estonia. Oleviste Church sat empty and deteriorated from years of neglect. Broken windows. Cracked plaster. Leaking roof. No heating system. Hundreds of birds and other creatures had made it their home. It was a desolate building in desperate shape. Truth be told, though, that was fine with Soviet leaders, since their anti-God thinking left no room for the Christian religion. In fact, they decided it was time to rid their region of much of the Christian influence, and they had a plan to do it.

Rather than simply wiping out the Christians, which would have created too much anti-Communist sentiment, they instead employed a tactic that had been used effectively in other parts of the Soviet Union. They would force the Christians of various backgrounds and denominations to work together. This would, in turn, cause the Christians to fight over theology. The churches, in effect, would destroy themselves. This method had been quite successful for the Communists in other places. As the Soviets simply sat back and watched, the Christians would argue over doctrines, and the churches fell apart. It was a very efficient technique.

With such a track record, this seemed like the best course of action to take in Tallinn. So the Soviets brought together the leaders of several different Christian churches of varying backgrounds — Baptist, Pentecostal, Free Evangelical, and more — and told them their buildings were being confiscated. They could all have, together, the one ancient, vacant, and dilapidated cathedral, but they would have to work cooperatively with one another. The Communists were sure this was the ticket to bringing an end to the majority of Christian influence in Tallinn.

Something went wrong with their plan, though. It didn't work quite the way they had expected. Much to the consternation of the Communists, the Christians in Tallinn actually willingly worked together. They set aside their theological differences and readily collaborated with each other. At their first combined service, there were 3,000 people in attendance that Sunday morning. That was an unprecedented show of solidarity. When people realized that it was nearly impossible to find a seat because of such a large crowd, it created real excitement. From that momentous beginning, many positive things happened.

I'm not suggesting that this melding of various churches together was a cakewalk. In fact, I was told it was very, very difficult. They had to walk through some extremely sticky situations. There were issues on which they clearly did not agree. Sometimes they even argued, yet the pastors willingly made concessions to one another. For example, they celebrated communion on different Sundays from two different traditions. They could easily have fought over which was right, but, instead, they chose to walk together, side by side, in love. They knew if they did not, then the Communists' plan would be successful. The church would be destroyed, and the enemy would have declared victory. So by the empowerment of the Spirit of Christ, they demonstrated that they were indeed Christ's followers by showing love toward one another.

This spirit of cooperation and giving place to one another confounded the Communists. They had never seen anything quite like it. They were certainly frustrated that their plan to rid Tallinn of much of the Christian influence had been foiled.

In many ways, Rein Uuemõis, not yet a pastor, guided the church through the amazing revival. When the Communists made their "work together" decree, he was a young member of one of the churches that was forced into this cooperative effort. Rein credits this initial collective working together as the necessary foundation for the revival. He clearly believes that if the churches had not been willing to work and walk together, the blessing of God would not have rested on the congregation in such a strong way. This idea certainly makes sense. After all, Psalm 133 says: "How good and pleasant it is when brothers dwell in unity... For there the LORD has commanded the blessing..."

Something happened as those pastors and churches worked together. Their cooperation set events in motion that would change the course of history.

Oskar Olvik had been the pastor of one of the churches that had been forced together. He later was officially named the senior pastor of Oleviste Church. Yet by 1969, Pastor Olvik was frustrated. Under Communist rule, evangelism of any sort was outlawed. Olvik saw people —

young people, especially — floundering under a Communistic mindset. He knew the Church had answers, but he also recognized that he could not readily offer those answers. The pressure from the Communists was too great. Students who displayed religious tendencies were confronted by school leadership. They were often forced to give an account of their actions. Although people were *allowed* to go to church, at the same time they were certainly *discouraged* from doing so. In a society that claimed there is no God, being religious was seen as an oddity at best... usually worse.

Someone studying for a teaching degree faced heightened persecution. Being a teacher in a Communist school and simultaneously having religious faith were viewed as completely incompatible. You could definitely not teach in a school if you were a practicing Christian. There was no leniency on that point.

Further, anyone who desired to enter the ministry could not receive any sort of formal theological training. Instead they would study something innocuous, engineering perhaps, to keep the authorities happy with them. They could then pursue biblical training in their spare time, in secret.

One former Estonian who was there during this time said, "Communism is an elaborate evil system. They plant informers in every strata of society... They use direct intimidation by making threats. If you don't cooperate with them, they can make your life miserable by taking away your promotion or education. And worst of all — they try to recruit you as an informer, trying to get you to betray your brothers — all the time they use psychological intimidation..."

The ongoing pressure to conform to the Communist agenda made life difficult at every turn. People always wondered who might be spying. *Is my neighbor, who acts very friendly, actually just trying to keep an eye on my activities for the Communists? Perhaps my coworker is really a government informant.* Such thoughts fostered a mindset of distrust.

It was not easy being a Christian in such a setting. Only those who were truly committed to their faith — those who were willing to pay the price — would regularly attend any type of religious meetings. Ülo Niinemägi, currently an assistant pastor at Oleviste, said it was physically hard. "You could almost feel the KGB squeezing you."

It was in this setting that Pastor Olvik decided something needed to change. He could not continue to stay silent while the state indoctrinated God out of the young people. He had the heart of an evangelist, and the Lord was gently, but firmly, nudging him to step out and evangelize. The question in Olvik's mind was, how could he do it without getting himself, his church, and the very people he was attempting to bring to Christ into too much trouble with the authorities?

One day he had an idea. Choir meetings. A choir performing modern music could be the avenue for evangelism. Sing some contemporary songs — Christian songs, of course — and then talk about what those songs meant.

Strengthen the faith of those who are already believers, and, at the same time, plant seeds into those who are not. Certainly the authorities couldn't get upset about people coming to be a part of — or even listen to — an innocuous church choir, could they? It was a brilliant God-idea that would have far-reaching ramifications for a very long time to come.

Under the Communists' rule, those who went to the Soviet Union to minister in a church, generally were only allowed to minister in the main church of their particular denomination. Almost exclusively, those primary churches were in Moscow, where the authorities could keep a watchful eye on the activities. Oleviste Church, after the merging of the churches of differing backgrounds, was declared to be a Baptist Church. The varying theologies of the different churches made no difference to the Communists. They wanted to give the church a label, and Baptist seemed like a good choice. So Oleviste was placed under the Baptist leaders in Moscow.

In Tallinn, though, there was a real oddity. It was a Methodist Church, located not far from Oleviste. There were almost no Methodist Churches throughout the entire Soviet Union at the time, and the main one happened to be located in Tallinn. That meant that if a minister, or even a musical ensemble, was allowed into the Soviet Union to minister in a Methodist Church, the one in Tallinn was the place they would go. This allowed that particular church a measure of freedom that didn't exist in most churches under the Communists.

It should be noted that when the Communists forced the other churches together, the Methodist Church remained separate. In fact, all the way back to the 1950s, the spiritual history of the church remained strong. There was a spiritual vitality at the church through the 1950s, 60s and into the 70s, that was, in some ways, a catalyst to the Oleviste revival. Each week on Thursday evening the Methodist Church had meetings that helped strengthen the faith of those attending. Separate from the Sunday services, these evening meetings were open to anyone, even people from other churches. Rein Uuemõis and his brother, Haljand, were frequent attenders.

In the very early 1970s, the focus of the meetings shifted somewhat, with more of an emphasis on the youth. Although the idea was somewhat similar to the meetings at Oleviste, the scope and vision were very different. Using first-rate performances of very contemporary music, they drew hundreds of people into the building. The church is located on Viru Square — in essence, the town square in Old Town Tallinn — and hundreds of people walked by each day on their way to work or to catch a tram or a bus. Rock music emanating from inside drew people in. They wanted to find out what was going on.

The time frame here should be noted carefully. In the early 1970s, even in the U.S., there were relatively few churches that were doing truly contemporary music.

For a church in Tallinn, Estonia, to be offering cutting-edge music at that time was monumental. At this time in Estonia, even secular music was distributed hand to hand, cassettes secretly copied, because they were not available any other way. So for a church to have music of the caliber being offered, available for free to anyone who wanted to come, was shocking. Non-Christians came simply because of the availability of free, high-quality contemporary music. Some secular musicians came because the church had somehow obtained really good-quality instruments — a Fender electric guitar, for example — and musicians just wanted to see such things in person. Every Thursday night hundreds of people came to hear and see what they could find nowhere else in Estonia.

These youth-focused meetings ended up drawing hundreds of people into the Kingdom of God. It was actually quite the phenomenon.

By the mid-70s, though, there came conflict within the church about those Thursday meetings. Some church members didn't like the style of music. Others were upset that although the kids made a commitment to the Lord, they made no commitment to the church. Still others thought it despicable that music was emphasized far more than theology. The feud was underway. Accusations were leveled and heated words exchanged. It was not a pretty sight. Brothers fought against brothers, all while God was drawing people into His Kingdom. Unfortunately, before all the dust settled from the arguing, most of the young people were gone from the Methodist Church.

They didn't want to be in the middle of the debate, so many of them left. However, in God's sovereignty, the majority of them landed at Oleviste.

———————————•••••••———————————

Pastor Olvik named his church choir Effataa. This is a transliteration of a word of Aramaic origin meaning "be opened." In the Gospel of Mark, Jesus spoke the word to a man who was deaf and who had a speech impediment. As soon as Jesus said it, the man's "ears were opened, his tongue was released, and he spoke plainly" (Mark 7:35). The apparent meaning, in regards to the choir meetings, was that the leaders were asking God to open the spiritual eyes and ears of those who attended the meetings. The name had nothing to do with any hopes for physical healing. Pastor Olvik's goal was purely evangelistic. He and the others who led the meetings simply wanted the Holy Spirit to open those eyes and ears that had not yet been opened to the gospel of the Lord Jesus Christ. With that purpose in mind, Effataa seemed like a good choice for a name.

Right from the beginning, Pastor Olvik knew that this could not be a traditional church choir. If they really wanted to have an impact on the young people, the music would need to be something to which young people could relate. The Methodist Church's contemporary music evenings certainly influenced the style that was used at Oleviste, yet the thrust of the meetings at Oleviste was decidedly different right from the beginning. Pastor Olvik put Rein Uuemõis in charge of the choir meetings. The plan was to bring together a core group of singers and instrumentalists. From there, he would encourage those people to invite their unsaved friends and family. Each evening they would sing the songs together — "rehearsing" — and then talk about the meanings of the songs. Of course, it would be necessary, in the context of the songs, to insert a presentation of the gospel into the talking time. It would seem natural, not forced. As the gospel was made clear and plain, Pastor Olvik and Rein both knew that people would respond. And they did.

The meetings began in the Oleviste vestry. It was a small room to the left of the altar area that could hold perhaps fifty people. It didn't take long, though, before they outgrew that room. When this happened, the meetings moved to the opposite side of the altar area, into Mary Chapel, a room that could easily hold a couple hundred people. New people kept coming, and at each meeting more and more people were born again. God was doing something miraculous.

Those Effataa Choir meetings actually began with more than just singers and instrumentalists. There were also prayer warriors. These were folks who had a heartfelt vision for the choir concept. It was an entire team dedicated to praying that the people — especially the young people — of Tallinn would come to know Christ. They prayed diligently for the meetings. They prayed for the people who would attend, that their hearts would be open to the Lord. They prayed for those who would lead and share at the meetings, that God would guide and direct them. They prayed for the Holy Spirit to touch hearts and draw lives to the living Christ. They prayed... and God answered.

Along with the prayers for the Effataa Choir meetings, there was also a pervasive, underlying hunger for God. I interviewed many of the people who were involved in those early meetings. The thing I heard over and over was that they were seeking God for more. As they read Scripture, they saw a qualitative difference between the picture presented there and the lives they were living. Inside them there grew an intense longing and hunger for the Lord Himself, a true desire to really know Him in tangible ways.

One man who was involved summarized this powerful drive in the words of Psalm 130: "Out of the depths I cry to you, O LORD! O Lord, hear my voice! Let your ears be attentive to the voice of my pleas for mercy... I wait for the LORD, my soul waits, and in his word I hope; my soul waits for the Lord more than watchmen for the morning, more than watchmen for the morning" (Psalm 130:1-2, 5-6). That was the yearning I heard echoed over and over.

The Holy Spirit clearly had placed within them an intense desire for God. Ask any of the people who were part of that early group, and they'll tell you it wasn't something they worked up in themselves. That hunger and passion were grace-gifts from the Lord Himself.

His Word declares: "You will seek me and find me,

when you seek me with all your heart. I will be found by you, declares the LORD..." (Jeremiah 29:13-14). The New Testament tells us that "he rewards those who seek him" (Hebrews 11:6), and that we should "draw near to God, and he will draw near to you" (James 4:8).

That's what a small group of believers at Oleviste did. They met together and prayed. They prayed for hours at a time. Frequently. Sometimes nightly. Their whole-hearted hunger for the Lord was so strong that they made a point of meeting together and seeking Him. It was not at all unusual for them to forgo their standard routines — birthdays and other celebrations, for example — to meet together for prayer. It was often declared during this time, "If you want an awakening, if you really desire for God to move in a powerful way among people, then you must forget about conveniences." And so they did. God, in turn, met them in ways beyond their expectations. He reward-ed the ones who were seeking Him.

One of the things I found fascinating during this time period was the strong commitment to holy living through confession of sin to one another. This idea, of course, is biblical. James 5:16, tells us, "Therefore, confess your sins to one another and pray for one another..."[2] And although this is clearly a scriptural mandate, it is rarely practiced throughout most of the Protestant Church. We tend to leave that to the Roman Catholics. The idea of verbally confessing our sins to another human being is generally uncomfortable for us.

The leaders at Oleviste, though, thought it was important. When they came together for prayer, they also took time to confess their sins to one another. From all I heard, they were apparently doing their utmost to maintain accountability, not only to God, but to one another. So, as they gathered to pray, they admitted their faults and sins. They shared sins of commission (anger, lustful thoughts, greed, etc.) and sins of omission (lack of prayer, etc.). They didn't want such things to be hidden but to be brought into the light. They took seriously Paul's admonition to the Church at Ephesus, "Take no part in the unfruitful works of darkness, but instead expose them" (Ephesians 5:11). Expose them they did.

As the leaders admitted their sins, they did as the Bible commands, they prayed for one another. They prayed for changed hearts and minds and lives. As evil was exposed, they prayed that God would replace that evil with the fruit of the Spirit. A God-exchange took place: His goodness for their unrighteousness.

The sermons that were shared during the revival services were primarily on the theme of renounce your sin and turn to Christ for forgiveness. In reality, that theme is heard repeatedly throughout the book of Acts. So, what the leaders were sharing was simply what they were living. They confessed that they were sinful, and prayed for the Lord to make changes in them, bringing them ever closer to the fullness of His image.

Without question, they would be quick to admit that they are all still far from perfect. Each of them still has struggles in their personal lives. At the same, time, though, they would also tell you that the confession of sins and prayer for one another made a big difference in them. In addition, they would say that it was one of the reasons God used them to help bring about the revival. †

Chapter 3

The Russians are Coming

As the meetings at Oleviste grew, people slowly began to come from farther and farther away. By 1977, the meetings were officially still labeled as the Effataa Choir meetings, but there was a stronger, bolder evangelistic thrust. The "choir" pretense was less evident, and the special three-per-month services had taken on a life of their own. In fact, some people had even been healed of physical illnesses during the services. Without the people seeking the miraculous, God had done the miraculous anyway. The leaders were as astounded as anyone by this turn of events.

Of course, the word of physical healings caused others to come. They wanted to see what was going on. Some also wanted to be healed. So the meetings that had once been attended almost exclusively by people from Tallinn, were now seeing visitors from other parts of Estonia and even other Soviet Bloc countries, especially Russia. In fact, by this time the meetings had ballooned to the point where Mary Chapel was no longer large enough to hold the crowds. They were forced to move into the main sanctuary.

I am keenly aware that over time memories fade. The revival took place more than thirty years ago. Recollections that were once vivid and clear can become clouded and muddled. Not everyone recalls the story I'm about to tell you, but two different eyewitnesses shared it with me, so I have to at least give it some credibility.

Each Saturday morning before the evening service, there was a prayer meeting at the home of Rein Uuemõis. At the time, he was still an engineer, not yet a pastor. Late in 1977, during one of those prayer meetings, Rein's phone rang. Someone was calling to let him know that hundreds of Russians had gathered around the church. They came from other parts of the Soviet Union and were there for the service, but it was still early in the day. The caller said that somebody needed to go unlock the church doors and let the people in.

Again, not everyone recalls that event, but, nevertheless, the attendance certainly kept growing. Russians came, but also Latvians, Lithuanians, Belarusians, Ukrainians and more. They came, hundreds and hundreds at a time. At each service, the sanctuary became more and more packed with people.

Keep in mind that this was 1977. There was no internet, no email capability. Also bear in mind that this was happening in Communist-controlled U.S.S.R. The church produced no advertisements or flyers. They couldn't afford to have that type of publicity. Although the services were growing, they still hoped to somehow stay beneath the radar of the government authorites. So any sort of written or broadcast advertisements were definitely not within the realm of possibility. Yet people came anyway, but not just from down the road. They came from all across the Soviet Union. Some came from near the Black Sea — more than 1,000 miles to the south — and others even from as far away as Kamchatka, Russia, (near Japan) — more than 4,000 miles to the east.

When the leaders at Oleviste began inquiring about how these folks knew to come to the church, some, of course, had heard about it from others. Many, though, gave a very different response. They had been given dreams and visions.

Please recognize that I am a pretty conservative guy. I do not have lots of experience in what many might call "the supernatural." I regularly minister in Mennonite and Lutheran and Baptist and Methodist churches. In those types of settings, I don't hear many people talking about having dreams and visions from God. At the same time, though, I am a firm believer in His Holy Word. In the second chapter of Acts, Peter quoted the prophet Joel: "And in the last days it shall be, God declares, that I will pour out my Spirit on all flesh... your young men shall see visions, and your old men shall dream dreams..." (Acts 2:17). Conservative background or not, it's right there in the Scripture, so I am forced to deal with it. Since God doesn't change (Malachi 3:6), dreams and visions are well within the realm of possibility for believers.

Those visitors from other countries told the leaders at Oleviste that they had received direction from God. Some had seen visions, others had dreams. But those dreams and visions all had one point. The people were told, "Go to Tallinn..." One woman who had such an experience admitted she didn't even know where Tallinn was. She thought it might be in Italy. "Go to Tallinn and go to the church with the very tall steeple." To this day, if you take a train from somewhere else to Tallinn, when you get off at the first stop in Tallinn and walk out the front door of the train station, you'll see Oleviste Church about a half-mile away. That gigantic steeple is unmistakable.

As I heard this same story from numerous people who were there, I was once again in awe of God's amazing mercy and sovereignty. He divinely directed people to go to a place where they could more fully encounter Him. Astounding!

The people coming from farther away obviously increased the total attendance. It also increased the number of people responding to the gospel. Whereas before there might have been as many as a dozen people who declared a first-time allegiance to Christ, from late in 1977 until October 1980 there were fifty or more people per service openly responding. That means thousands of people were born-again during that time frame. Actually, these numbers are on the conservative side. Some people I talked with say the totals were considerably higher. The unfortunate truth is that almost no records were kept about anything during the revival. Such records *couldn't* be kept because of the Communists. The believers did not want the secret police — or any other government official — to get their hands on anything that had names or specific information about what happened at the church. We'll never know for sure how many people received new life at the revival at Oleviste, but it's safe to say there were thousands who came into the Kingdom of God as a result of this God-event.

The truth is that the welcoming of the Russians was, in many ways, every bit as much a miracle as the salvations and healings that happened. Of course, unless you happen to be up on Estonian history, you likely would not understand why I would make such a statement. So let me explain.[1]

Estonia was controlled by the Russian Empire from

the mid-1800s until 1920. As a result, there is a very long history of anti-Russian sentiment. This underlying attitude was heightened even more through later events.

After gaining independence at the end of World War I, Estonia developed a high literacy rate and a strong economy. But in 1939 Hitler and Stalin signed the German-Soviet Nonaggression Pact (Molotov-Ribbentrop Pact), a military agreement between the Nazis and Soviets. This pact contained a secret clause that divided much of Europe between them. Estonia was promised to Russia. Just a few short days after the signing, more than 25,000 Russian soldiers invaded Estonia. Within months, thousands of Estonian citizens were executed, and many more just disappeared. Russia's leader, Joseph Stalin, once said that death solves all problems. "No person, no problem." It was a simple mantra by which the tyrannical dictator ruled.

Nearly anyone of influence — teacher, scientist, writer, politician — was killed. In a single night, 10,000 men, women, and children were wrenched from their homes, loaded into cattle cars, and taken to slave labor camps in Siberia. More than half of those people never returned.

The Estonian people lived in fear. Would they be next? Would they hear the knock on their own doors in the middle of the night, only to be ripped from their homes and killed or sent away to the gulag, the concentration camps? No one knew for sure.

Local Soviet officials would seize any convenient person to fulfill their ongoing prisoner quotas. Fully one-third of those who were deported to Siberia were children. One woman who was taken as a small girl said she got up one morning to go to school, just like usual. She was supposed to have a piano recital that day. Then she found herself in a cage like an animal. It all seemed surreal, as though she was dreaming.

Most of the time, those who were left behind received no information. They had no idea why their parents, grandparents, aunts, uncles, sisters, brothers, or children were taken away. Their questions were met with silence... or worse.

Shortly after the initial invasion, the Russians displayed their might by sending an additional 90,000 troops. That meant there was one Russian soldier for every nine Estonian citizens. What could the Estonian people do against such a formidable force?

That first year of Russian occupation became known in Estonia as "the year of suffering." The idea behind such a reign of terror was to destroy any and all resistance to the Russian occupation. It was very effective.

Then, in 1941, Hitler betrayed his agreement with Stalin. German forces invaded Russia and also Estonia. Estonian young men were forced to either join the German army or be shot. Anyone who had cooperated openly with the Russians was executed.

Just a few short years later, though, the war had turned yet again. Russian troops returned with a vengeance. They once again invaded Estonia, and all those who had cooperated with the Germans became the new targets.

It is estimated that during this time, 70,000 Estonians fled the country. They recalled the "year of suffering" and wanted no part of a repeat performance. Escape efforts, though, were not easy. Some drowned when their small boats sank. Others were killed by Russian planes. Still others were captured.

As this was happening, Stalin convinced Western leaders that he would soon hold free elections in Estonia. Believing Stalin, those Western leaders — Roosevelt, Churchill, and others — agreed to allow the continued occupation of Estonia. The nation was devastated. In those six years — 1939-1945 — between the executions, deportations, and refugees who fled, Estonia lost one-fourth of its population.

When the occupation of Estonia was complete and firm, there came an intense "Russification." In an attempt to completely eradicate any thoughts of Estonia as a nation, tens of thousands of Russian citizens were relocated there. Sometimes they formed entirely new cities. Other times they just moved in right next door to Estonian citizens. Farms were confiscated from their owners and "collectivized." Those who resisted were arrested and banished to Siberia. Anything reminiscent of free Estonian life was destroyed. Estonia, for all practical purposes, no longer existed. It was now a Soviet Socialist Republic.

All of this clearly intensified the Estonians' already overwhelming distrust, and even hatred of Russians. The Estonians despised the Russian government and their newly imported Russian neighbors. It was a deep-seated animosity that lasted all the way until Estonia gained freedom in 1991. Truthfully, in many Estonians who remember, this animosity is still present today.

So the fact that the leaders of the revival at Oleviste not only allowed, but welcomed the Russians is amazing. They ultimately ended up having special Russian services on Saturday afternoons. Everything spoken and sung in those services was in Russian, as opposed to the Estonian language used for the main services. But the Oleviste leaders even offered translation of the regular revival services into Russian, so their visitors could understand what was being said. A sophisticated (at least for that time) network of headphones was incorporated to help the Russians to be able to participate. There was no, "You're not welcome here," attitude that pervaded so much of the rest of the Estonian society. No, Oleviste welcomed the Russians with open arms.

Part of this welcoming of the Russians was due to Rein. Earlier in his life, Rein had spent time in Russia, studying. Some of his classmates there were predictably very rude toward him; boys will be boys. However, he lived for a time with a family who treated him as though he was their stepson. It was thanks to them that Rein got to meet and appreciate the Russian people. As a result, he harbored no animosity in his heart toward Russians. So he gladly welcomed them when they came to Oleviste.

Considering the general underlying hostility toward the Russian people throughout Estonia, this is clearly another miracle from the hand of God. In a very real way, they were truly able to love their enemies. The earlier merging of various Christian churches from very different backgrounds and then the welcoming of the much-despised Russians — both of these were major building blocks that the Lord used to help bring about this amazing revival.

———————————————————

The title of this chapter is "The Russians Are Coming" but there was another phenomenon that happened as the Russians returned home. As I interviewed various people who had been in some leadership capacity during the Oleviste revival services, the stories were rampant of entire Russian villages that were affected. Someone, or several someones, came to the church and were born-again or physically healed. When they went back, others were impacted in the same way. Families, and even whole towns, received the good news and the miraculous touch of God.

Additionally, many of those who were in leadership roles during the revival went out and ministered in churches across the Soviet Union. The Lord had spurred their faith by what they saw in Tallinn, and He used them as instruments to touch many thousands more who never actually visited Oleviste. The revival spread, and the influence was felt in nearly every corner of the Soviet Union.

Just from the people I spoke with directly, I heard the stories of at least a hundred churches that were started as a direct result of the revival. People have told me firsthand of churches begun in Latvia, Lithuania, Ukraine, Belarus, and all across Russia. Additionally, I know of Russian churches scattered across the U.S. — from California, Oregon, and Washington to Georgia and Florida — that trace their roots to the revival at Oleviste Church. Honestly, I know I have only scratched the surface. It is likely that if I continued searching (sorry, too much time and money to do this), I would find several hundred churches directly linking their beginnings to the revival in Tallinn, Estonia. International evangelist Slavik Radchuk says he knows of two-hundred churches in the U.S. alone that would trace their origins back to the Oleviste revival. These are the miracles brought about by the sovereign hand of God.

Beyond the churches that were begun as a result of this awakening, others were bolstered. As the Holy Spirit infused the lives of believers at Oleviste Church, they returned to their respective churches and brought new life and vitality. Hundreds upon hundreds of churches were made stronger and more vibrant as the Lord touched people's lives in powerful and profound ways.

Recently I was teaching a Worship Seminar in Connersville, Indiana. Connersville is not exactly a major metropolitan area. During the seminar, I mentioned the Oleviste revival in the context of my teaching. It was simply an illustration about the churches working together. After the seminar, a woman approached me. She was, perhaps, in her early twenties, and, in a strong Slavic accent, she told me that she was from Siberia. Her father is now a

Christian pastor in Siberia. But in the late 1970s, before she was born, he had been physically healed in Oleviste Church.

This Great Soviet Awakening was quite possibly the biggest and most widespread revival of the twentieth century. The effects reached every part of the Soviet Union and even worldwide. Even more amazing is the fact that it happened under persecution in a nation whose government declared that God does not exist. †

Chapter 4

The Miracles

Udo Veevo pastored a church on the island of Hiuma, an Estonian island in the Baltic Sea. Pastor Veevo had heard about what was happening at Oleviste, but he was skeptical. Because of this, he personally went to check it out. He wanted to see firsthand whether this work was truly from God. When he went to a service, he decided it must be of God, because the gospel was clearly preached and people openly repented of their sins. He believed if people were acknowledging that they were sinful, it could only be the Holy Spirit who caused such a recognition. After all, Jesus plainly declared: "And when he (the Holy Spirit) comes, he will convict the world concerning sin and righteousness and judgment" (John 16:8).

Peeter Püssim was there from the beginning of the revival. He said the messages that were shared were simple: Jesus loves you, repent and receive Him, He will make you new. It was a clear and straightforward presentation of the gospel.

Rein Uuemõis says that the primary emphasis during the revival was on relationship with God. His main message was repentance from sin and receiving forgiveness through Christ's atoning sacrifice. He insisted that there be a Godward focus in a person's life before praying for healing. From what I heard directly from Rein, as well as from others with whom I spoke, Rein's first priority was evangelism. He wanted every person who attended the services to be in right relationship with the Lord.

I personally find it amazing that the Communists allowed them to give altar calls. This seems completely contrary to everything I have read and heard of this era in the Soviet Union. It also seems contradictory, because not much later the Soviets refused to allow such a thing. Billy Graham spoke at Oleviste Church in 1984. People packed into every corner of nearly every room in the building. More than 4,000 people were in attendance at that meeting. Oddly, he was allowed to speak only after he agreed to not offer an altar call, a hallmark of his ministry. Yet, just a few years earlier, that same approach to evangelism was happening regularly at Oleviste. For some apparently miraculous reason that only God knows, the leaders of the revival were allowed to evangelize in ways that weren't normally accepted by the Communists.

As the meetings grew, some of the local people would go early and save seats for their friends. The front rows filled up quickly as a result. The leaders at Oleviste did not want this to happen. Their goal was to see people saved. They knew their goal was not to try to evangelize Christians. They wanted those who were not yet born-again filling the pews during these meetings, so at some point (no one is quite sure of the date, because of the lack of recordkeeping) they instituted a policy that said local believers must have an unsaved person with them in order to enter. Of course, that made some people upset. Some of the locals made it known that they were not happy about this new rule. The believers wanted to hear the messages and see what was happening, the salvations and healings. They wanted to be a part of the meetings. However, the whole point of why these meetings began was to reach the lost, so the leaders kept faithful to that original vision.

I already mentioned that records of salvations were not kept. Those countless salvations, though, were the biggest miracles that God did during the revival. Between the beginnings of the revival at the Methodist Church, then on to the Effataa Choir meetings, and, finally, to the multitudes pouring in from across the Soviet Union, thousands upon thousands of people were born-again. Legitimate estimates range from 10,000 to more than 20,000 salvations.[1] Those souls will be in heaven forever, as a result of what the Lord did in Tallinn, Estonia, during those years from the early 1970s through 1980.

Recently I had the privilege of meeting Slavik Radchuk. He is a native of Ukraine now living in Atlanta, Georgia. Slavik is an evangelist who has ministered in more than seventy nations. Hundreds of thousands of people have been born-again as a result of his ministry. He has personally helped start hundreds of churches worldwide.

As I talked with Slavik, he told of having visited Oleviste Church during the revival. At the time he was just a teenager. He was already a Christian, but it was at Oleviste that God graced him with the power of the Holy Spirit and the gift of an evangelist. The leaders at the church recognized the gift of God in his life, and they prayed over him. Slavik became one of just a handful of people who was officially sent out from Oleviste to help take what God was doing into other parts of the Soviet Union. He traveled throughout the Soviet Bloc countries and saw thousands of new converts as result. Slavik was constantly harassed by the secret police as he moved about. Still, in 1983, at the age of just twenty-four, he took a group of twenty young evangelists into Siberia. He was not deterred by the threats of the Soviet secret police. The Lord had seemingly made him fearless in following the call of God.

Slavik told me of one service where he and his ministry partner both sensed a need to leave town immediately after the service. Although it was Saturday evening, and they were planning to minister again at the church on Sunday morning, they both felt it best to depart as quickly as possible. So, as soon as the Saturday evening service ended, they asked their host, the church's pastor, to take them to the train station. He did his best to dissuade them from going, but they were adamant. The pastor finally agreed and drove them to the station. Just that quickly, they were gone. Later they found out that government agents had arrived at the church right after the pastor returned. The secret police wanted to arrest Slavik and his traveling companion. The Lord miraculously rescued them from the oppressors.

When the Iron Curtain fell, Slavik found new freedom to minister. With the Soviet persecutors no longer holding sway, doors opened in amazing new ways. Since then, and continuing through to today, he has had the opportunity to take the gospel message to literally millions of people around the globe. It is one more tremendous ray of light that resulted from the revival at Oleviste Church.

———————————————— •••◉••• ————————————————

For many of the people who were there, the physical healings that happened were the most tangible of the Lord's miracles. Seeing someone suddenly and visibly healed and restored obviously made for a very memorable experience.

The Oleviste leadership did their best to follow a biblical pattern as they ministered. They brought people to a point of confessing their sins and then prayed for healing. "Therefore, confess your sins to one another and pray for one another, that you may be healed" (James 5:16). Of course, just prior to that verse, James declared: "Is anyone among you sick? Let him call for the elders of the church, and let them pray over him, anointing him with oil in the name of the Lord. And the prayer of faith will save the one who is sick, and the Lord will raise him up" (James 5:14-15). Following this scriptural mandate, the leaders of the revival prayed. The result was that people were healed, just like God promised in His Word.

The leaders almost never requested, or even allowed, immediate testimonies of healings during the meetings. They wanted to be sure that the experience wasn't just an emotionally-charged, temporary feeling. The Oleviste leaders wanted reality, not just sensationalism. Testimonies that were given at another time — perhaps the next service, or sometime later — were encouraged because they demonstrated that the Lord had indeed done a work in the person.

As you read these stories, please keep in mind that neither Pastor Oskar Olvik — the one who started the choir meetings — or Rein Uuemõis — the man who guided the church through the revival — were from a Pentecostal background. Oleviste was not a Pentecostal Church. Olvik and Uuemõis were both originally from a Free Evangelical background. Some of the other leaders there had been Baptist. One of the key people in the revival was from a Lutheran background. These were not Pentecostals. On the other hand, one man I interviewed, Janis Ozolikievts, was from a strongly Pentecostal background. His first experience at Oleviste immediately made him dubious. Janis' Pentecostal upbringing had taught him how to pray "correctly." When he prayed for people, they knew they had been prayed for, even if nothing happened immediately. His praying was lengthy and loud and boisterous. No genteel prayers from this man. That's just not the way it was done. If prayer was to be offered publicly, the public was going to hear it.

Such a mindset was the reason Janis was skeptical when he visited Oleviste for the first time. He didn't think that Baptists — the official label given by the Communists — knew how to pray correctly. And, from his perspective, his initial visit to Oleviste gave him good reason for thinking that way. None of the leaders had ever heard anyone shouting a prayer. Such an idea had never even crossed their minds. So when those leaders at Oleviste prayed, they generally prayed short, simple, and even soft-spoken prayers. They didn't yell. Sometimes they were barely audible. Janis Ozolikievts was certain that God could not work through such prayers. But He did. Over and over again, He did.

One night a Ukrainian father brought his 12-year-old son to the meeting. The boy was deaf and mute; couldn't hear, couldn't speak. The father and son had come to the service with several other people from their village in Ukraine. After the main meeting, prayer was being offered in Mary Chapel. When it was time for prayers for healing the sick, the father took his son and got into one of the prayer lines. They patiently waited their turn, but when Rein and Enno Tuulik prayed, nothing happened. The boy remained exactly as he had been: deaf and mute. The father and son walked away, somewhat dejectedly.

A woman from their village was in the same line, and she let the dad and boy take her spot in the prayer line. She apparently thought the boy's need was greater than her own. Again, the two slowly inched their way forward until they reached the front of the line, and, once again, they requested prayer. Rein was not pleased that they had returned again — especially since many other people had not yet been prayed for at all. Nevertheless, he and Enno prayed again, but again nothing happened. The father and son stepped away. Yet, once again, there was another person from their village in the same line. That man also allowed the two to take his place in line. So, like the last two times, they slowly made their way to the front.

This time, when Rein recognized them, he was almost ready to refuse to pray. In his mind, he thought, "You are cheating. This is not a market; it is the house of God. We have prayed, so you should go." But he didn't say any of those things. Instead, he looked at Enno and said, "Again he is here! What should we do?" Enno responded, "Let's pray." So they prayed a third time, but, once again, seemingly nothing happened. The man and his son walked away once more. This time, though, they did not get back into the line. Instead, they began to leave. When they reached the door of Mary Chapel, though, the boy who had been deaf and mute stopped, looked at his father, and said in a loud voice, "Papa, let's go home." Two weeks later nearly their entire Ukrainian village was at the service at Oleviste.

Helio Leah was 75 years old when I met her. She had been born-again under the ministry of Pastor Udo Veevo, on the island of Hiuma. At the time of our meeting, she seemed frail, and I would have guessed her age to be more than 75. At the same time, though, Helio radiated Christ. Her eyes sparkled. Her smile was infectious. She said that many people have commented to her that she must have been blessed by God. The truth is that she has. Yet, during the time of the revival, Helio was diagnosed with uterine cancer (now commonly called endometrial cancer). For a woman in her mid-forties to receive a diagnosis of cancer must have been a devastating experience. Remember, this was the late 1970s, not today. Cancer research was nowhere close to the level we have now, especially in the Soviet Union. In most instances, their medical practices lagged many years behind the West. Cancer, in that era, would usually be the equivalent of a death sentence.

Helio had been to Oleviste several times, but this time she went and requested prayer. She wanted to be healed of the cancer. The brothers there prayed for her, and Helio was instantly and completely cured. The doctors who examined her later were amazed that she showed no sign of the cancer, and they gave her a clean bill of health.

Helio also told me about something else that happened beyond the walls of Oleviste. As a result of her healing, her daughters — then ages eight and eleven — turned to the Lord for forgiveness and salvation. The salvations had taken place more than thirty years prior to my interviewing her, but she was still visibly moved at the remembrance.

Once while Janis Ozolikievts was praying for others with Alexander Popov, a man approached them for prayer. Before they had a chance to pray or even talk to the man, Alexander looked at him and said, "You are a thief!" Janis was amazed at Alexander's boldness. Alexander then proceeded to list many of the things the man had stolen, some very specific. God gave him precise details about the exact items this man had pilfered. The man admitted that it was all true and that Alexander was correct about what he had stolen. "What should I do now?" the man asked. They responded that he needed to repent and stop stealing.

One woman told of a friend, an Estonian young lady, who had a hemangioma, a large purple-red splotch that covered half her face. Although the woman who shared the story considered the young lady with the ailment a friend, she referred to her as being "very ugly" as a result of the skin condition. The leaders at Oleviste prayed for the young lady, and she received, as the woman who related the story phrased it, "brand new skin." The splotch was completely gone, and new, flesh-colored skin replaced what had been purple-red.

At one meeting, an older girl — likely a teen — who had been crippled, was healed. She laid down her crutches — her only means of getting around for more than a decade — and began running back and forth in Mary Chapel. After noting the girl huffing and puffing, Rein cautioned her mother to not allow her to tire herself out for no reason. The mother, laughing and crying at the same time, responded, "She hasn't taken a single unassisted step in more than ten years. Let her practice!"

A woman came to the church from Russia. She said that her son was a doctor and that she had a "heart disease." Her son had been treating her for quite some time using various methods, all to no avail. She was prayed for that night, and she went home. Some weeks later a letter of thanks arrived. The woman expressed her deepest gratitude to God for what He had done through the prayers at Oleviste. She described her son's amazement when he realized that she was completely healed. He promised to go to Tallinn to find out what miraculous means they used to heal people.

One memorable Saturday evening for Rein was the night he met a man named Peter. Peter suffered from elephantiasis. This is a terrible disease that is characterized by the gross enlargement of a limb or areas of the trunk or head. There is an abnormal accumulation of watery fluid in the tissues (edema) causing severe swelling. Usually the skin develops a thickened, pebbly appearance and may become ulcerated and darkened. It is not only a debilitating disease, but the afflicted person can look gruesome.

One glance at Peter caused Rein to wonder, "What am I going to do?" He had never before encountered anything quite like this. So Rein chose to do what he always did, pray. "I laid my hand on him, and he began to shake so strongly that I thought his head would come off." In a few moments the man calmed down, but Rein didn't see any apparent change in his appearance. When the Saturday night service ended, the man left.

Sunday, though, the man came back to the church to give testimony. He was completely healed. There was absolutely no evidence at all of the illness. During the service, Peter shared the rest of the story. He had been on his way to see an expensive doctor in Moscow, when he met some believers from Ukraine on a train. Peter hoped the doctor would be able to offer him a cure, yet it was likely going to cost far more than he could afford. The believers asked him, "Why are you going to Moscow to spend money? Go with us to Oleviste Church in Tallinn, and get healed for free." And so he did. He definitely felt that God's method not only cost him less money, but it was also much quicker.

I heard several other amazing stories of "chance" encounters on trains, either going to or leaving Oleviste. One of the most memorable was the story of a man whose wife had a disease that left her incapacitated. She was so weak she could not walk. He was a very big man and she a small woman, so he carried her in a blanket slung over his back. It seemed like the most practical way for him to transport his feeble wife. They took a train from somewhere in Russia to Tallinn, Estonia, in hopes that she would be healed. Unfortunately, when the brothers at Oleviste prayed, nothing happened. The next day the couple — the husband still carrying the wife in the blanket — dejectedly boarded the train to go back home. During the trip, their fellow passengers saw the wife's condition. They knew she was not well. So when the woman suddenly stood up, completely healed, the other travelers insisted on knowing more about the church where they had been. Apparently God waited to heal her so that it would happen in front of non-believing witnesses on the train.

As I listened to the stories of what the Lord did, one of the things that gave me pause was the mention of prayer cloths. Apparently people from all across the Soviet Union came and laid handkerchiefs and scarves on the grand piano in Mary Chapel. The leaders of the revival then prayed over these cloths and sent them home with the people. As a result, testimonies were received from all parts of the U.S.S.R. about healings that happened because of the prayer cloths.

Again, this whole idea is a bit "out there" in my mind. Praying over a piece of cloth and having God, then, somehow heal someone as a result seems... well, strange to me. If I am honest, though, I have to admit that this idea is not without scriptural precedent. "And God was doing extraordinary miracles by the hands of Paul, so that even handkerchiefs or aprons that had touched his skin were carried away to the sick, and their diseases left them and the evil spirits came out of them" (Acts 19:11-12). Whether I am comfortable with the idea or not, it happened in Scripture. Why, then, should I suggest that such a thing is not possible in modern times? If I am honest, I must admit that it, indeed, could be possible.

I heard several stories about the prayer cloths, but one of the most amazing came from a Russian-language DVD series about the revival in Tallinn. Through a translator, I found that, although the series was produced in Russian, it was made here in the United States. Toward the end of the third and final DVD, Ekaterina Pekun, an elderly woman from Russia who now lives in California, shared an amazing story.

It was harvest time in the late 1970s. Ekaterina and her family lived on a farm in a rural area of Russia. During the harvest, her sons, Sasha and Viktor, were moving hay using pitchforks. Sasha was apparently not paying attention and accidently jabbed his pitchfork right into Viktor's face. One tine entered just below his eye, and another pierced his nose. The face of the eleven-year-old boy bled profusely and began to swell around the wounded area.

The family rushed Viktor to the local doctor, who immediately got him onto an airplane bound for Minsk, the nearest large city. The loss of blood and the inordinate amount of swelling caused the local doctor to believe that only the treatment he could receive in a big-city hospital would save him. So Viktor was whisked away to Minsk.

At his bedside in the hospital, his mother prayed and encouraged Viktor to pray also. Someone who had just returned from Oleviste Church brought in one of those handkerchiefs that had been prayed over. They carefully laid the cloth on the young boy's face. The next morning, there was no more bleeding and no signs that he had even been wounded. Not the slightest indication of the punctures or scars remained. Viktor was totally and completely healed. The doctors were astonished at such a clearly miraculous turn of events. After checking him thoroughly, they released him from the hospital.

Although no official records were kept of what happened during the services, it was found later that, for a short period of time, one man secretly recorded some of the testimonies. As people shared what the Lord had done, he used a small portable cassette recorder to capture the testimony. Later, back at his apartment, he wrote out the testimonies, including the dates of when they were given. He began keeping the records in September, 1978, and the final entry date is from April of 1979, just a brief eight-month period of time. I was privileged to receive a copy of that document. There were more than one-hundred testimonies. With so many amazing stories, it was difficult to decide which ones to include. Following is just a small sampling of those stories.

A nurse from Russia came to the meeting on Saturday, October 7, 1978. She had a small tumor on her wrist that had been diagnosed as malignant. The doctors had operated, but the surgery was unsuccessful. Her hand and wrist had become very sensitive to cold. As a result, her hand was bandaged and covered with a wool mitten, even indoors. The brothers at Oleviste prayed for her, and the next day she returned with her hand uncovered to say that the tumor was completely gone.

In November of 1978, a 60-year-old woman came from somewhere in Russia, hundreds of kilometers away. Seventeen years previously she had fallen and apparently broken her hip. She never received proper medical treatment, so her hip joints and pelvis had grown together and become fused. Several doctors had tried to help over the years, but none made any tangible difference. In fact, the last doctor had performed an operation, put her in a cast, and prescribed six months of lying in bed in the cast. It did absolutely no good. When she came to the service, she had great difficulty walking, and she managed only with the help of a cane. She shared that, as the brothers prayed, she was healed. Something on the inside changed, and she could walk just fine. She shouted, "Hallelujah! Thank You, Jesus!" She left her cane there at the altar in Mary Chapel, and returned to her home, healed.

That same evening, two brothers came, also from Russia. They had come to request prayer for their father, who was back at their home, dying of throat cancer. According to the brothers, their father's cancer had developed to a point where he could no longer swallow food.

They knew he could not last much longer without eating. So they asked for and received prayer for his healing. The next evening they returned to the church. With tears in their eyes, they testified that their father had been cured. They had spoken on the phone saying, "He can eat and feels much better." They verbalized their gratefulness to God and their appreciation for the prayers. They said, "He can cure even from a thousand kilometers away!"

In December of 1978, a letter was shared from a mother who lived near the Black Sea. She wrote that she and her daughter had recently been to a service at Oleviste Church. The daughter's eyes were very weak, and she wore extremely thick glasses. The girl was prayed for that night. As a result, her eyes were healed, and she could see perfectly without the aid of the glasses. Because of the healing, they had left the glasses there on the altar in Mary Chapel.

Also in December, 1978, some parents brought their 10-year-old son to one of the services. His feet were underdeveloped, and he could not walk at all. After a short prayer, he cautiously took a few steps. Finding he was able to do that, he started to walk back and forth. His parents thanked and praised God, shedding tears of joy for their son's healing.

That same month, an Estonian man testified that he had had chronic rhinitis since he was a small child. I'll be honest. I had no idea what that was, so I did a bit of research. Turns out that rhinitis is nasal dripping because of inflammation. The causes can be as varied as viruses, bacteria, or even irritants or allergies. So *chronic* rhinitis means that this guy's nose was running all the time. Nonstop. The man said he had tried doctors and medicines for years, and nothing had helped. But that night they prayed, and the Great Physician healed him.

On a Sunday in January of 1979, a woman from Russia gave this testimony: "My right ear has not heard anything since I was a child. Last night when the brothers prayed for me, my ear was healed, and now I can hear with it completely normally. The Holy Spirit has touched me, and I can go home as a new person. I thank God that He has been so good to me."

During a service in February, 1979, a letter from a woman from Ivanovo, Russia (nearly 1,000 kilometers — or 620 miles — away), was shared during a service. "I am 20 years old, and I suffered from serious renal pelvis disease (a rare kidney cancer) and pyelitis (inflammation of the renal pelvis). I spent a month in a local hospital with the disease, where I was treated, but with no results. After that, I went to Oleviste Church, where I was healed through the power of prayer. Now I thank God, because I feel healthy and like a new person."

On Sunday, March 25, 1979, an older woman testified, "I came here with two crutches. I was crippled, and I could barely walk. On Saturday, as I was praying before the meeting, I felt my feet were healing. I gave up the crutches, and I could move freely. I went up and down the stairs forty times and was convinced that God had healed my legs. Praise His Name!"

Also in March of 1979, a woman shared a testimony

from a friend of hers. They were from Alma-Ata, Kazakhstan, nearly 3,000 kilometers (more than 1,800 miles) from Tallinn. The friend, a mother, had brought her deaf daughter to Oleviste for prayer. The brothers had prayed for her, but seemingly nothing had happened. The mother and girl left, dejectedly, for their long journey home. On the train, the mother shared with fellow travelers how they had gone to Oleviste for prayer, but nothing happened. As she said this, her daughter spoke up, "Mom, I can hear everything you say very well!"

That same month, a man came to a Sunday meeting. After the meeting, the man went and sat down next to the preacher. He said that he was a driver for a school for the blind. Three weeks earlier, a blind girl from the school had come to the service. When she arrived back home, she was able to see perfectly. She stayed at the school only to finish the school term and then began studies at a new school. The man said that the girl's healing had a huge effect on the school. Additionally, besides the girl herself, her mother, father, sister, and brothers all became believers, as a result of her sight being restored.

Again, these are just a few of the amazing testimonies recorded and transcribed during that eight-month window in the late 1970s.

I met and interviewed Ivi Rang at her home. She was a vivacious woman in her forties. Ivi had been born-again as a teenager during the revival.

As she shared her recollections of the revival, she told of nights when "tears covered the altar railing" as a result of people kneeling and repenting of their sins. She said that she usually had prayed with her eyes closed, but when she began to hear the testimonies of people who had been healed, she admitted that she kept her eyes open more often because she wanted to see for herself what happened. As a reult, Ivi saw some amazing healings there at Oleviste.

When she became a Christian, Ivi had no Bible. Their family had no religious books at all. Because of this, she had nothing to read for spiritual nourishment. The only real spiritual "food' she received was from the sermons during church services. She went to the meetings at the Methodist Church, as well as those at Oleviste.

Ivi desperately wanted a Bible, so she began to pray for one. She wanted to read the Word of God for herself. It was just after she began to pray that a friend loaned her a Bible. Ivi was ecstatic. She could finally read it on her own, and she did. She read and read.

Keep in mind that she was a new believer. Pretty much all she knew of church life — the majority of her religious experience — was what she had seen and heard at Oleviste. As Ivi began reading through the gospels, she thought, *This is exactly what I see happening at church. The messages are simple. Blind people see. Lame people walk. Sick people are healed.* None of what she read surprised her, because it was just what she had experienced. Sometime later she was quite astonished, and even shocked, to find that this was not the norm at most churches. During the revival, Baptist leaders came from Leningrad (now St. Petersburg) to visit. They wanted to see what was going on at Oleviste. They were there to check out the validity of what was happening at the church. After being in one of the revival services, those leaders concluded that it was all wrong. The salvations and healings, in their estimation, were not from God. Yet they saw at each service, dozens of people who repented and trusted Christ as their Savior. Dozens of others were prayed for and instantly healed. Regardless of that fact, the Leningrad leaders had rendered their judgment, even though they had no scriptural basis for such a conclusion.

As I heard this same story from a few different people, I couldn't help remembering the words of Jesus to John's disciples: "Go and tell John what you have seen and heard: the blind receive their sight, the lame walk, lepers are cleansed, and the deaf hear, the dead are raised up, the poor have good news preached to them" (Luke 7:22).

Rein calls the revival time "normal church life." He clearly believes it should be that way all the time. In essence, it's just like the book of Acts, and it parallels Jesus' ministry.

Perhaps Ivi's perspective — that what happened at Oleviste looked pretty normal compared with Scripture — was correct. After all, Scripture clearly tells us that: "Jesus Christ is the same yesterday and today and forever" (Hebrews 13:8). He hasn't changed. But maybe we have. †

Chapter 5

Why It Began, Why It Ended

As I heard this story for the first time, I couldn't help wonder how it could have happened. From all I knew of that era, the idea seemed preposterous. After all, I have a few friends who actually smuggled Bibles into Communist countries during this same time period. It was a difficult and dangerous task to sneak "contraband" — illegal goods, like Bibles and other Christian literature — into closed, Soviet-controlled countries. They told me firsthand of clandestine rendezvous in out-of-the-way places with unknown people. For the sake of the church there, a certain level of secrecy had to be maintained even when they came back home. They shared about the perils and dangers of being caught. Christianity was not welcomed in the U.S.S.R. Actually, the Soviet authorities hoped to expunge the Christian faith from their nation. So how, then, could a revival — and one of such gigantic proportions — happen *within* the Soviet Union? I couldn't help being shocked by the entire prospect.

Please recognize that this all happened well before Mikhail Gorbachev, General Secretary of the Communist Party of the Soviet Union, implemented *perestroika* (restructuring) and *glasnost* (open discussion of political and social issues). According to both the historical information and stories I've heard personally, this should not have been possible. Christians were persecuted. Evangelism was banned. Christian literature of practically any type had been outlawed. The Christian religion in general was minimized at nearly every turn. How could a revival like this occur in the face of such opposition?

I posed that same question to nearly every person I interviewed in Estonia. These were all people who were present at or near the beginning of the revival. Although some didn't have any ideas at all, others gave some very thought-provoking answers.

First, the primary and most common explanation I heard is simply that God is sovereign. It was His idea. There was no reason, in the natural, that He should look upon Tallinn, or even specifically Oleviste Church, as anything special, yet He apparently did. Rein Uuemõis said, "The revival was a gift of grace we didn't expect." Ultimately, God is in control. "Whatever the LORD pleases, he does, in heaven and on earth..." (Psalm 135:6). God "does according to his will among the host of heaven and among the inhabitants of the earth; and none can stay his hand or say to him, 'What have you done?'" (Daniel 4:35). The Lord is sovereign. He does what He pleases.

In his commentary on the book of *Exodus*, John I. Durham made an interesting statement.

> By revealing himself as 'I AM WHO I AM' the Lord had in effect said, 'Yes, I have committed myself to you to be actively present with you, but I am not at your unfettered disposal. My active presence is mine and mine alone to exercise when and under what conditions I choose.[1]

The Lord can do anything He wants. If He wants to give an unexpected "gift of grace" to people suffering under the oppressive hand of Communism in the Soviet Union, who are we to argue? Some said that the revival occurred merely because of the sovereignty of God. From all I saw and heard, they seem to have a strong case for that opinion.

Another reason the revival happened is because of the various churches that were thrust together. Although they were all Christians, they were from very different theological persuasions. Conservative evangelicals to

Pentecostals, their doctrinal differences were not insignificant. Rein Uuemõis recalls that initially working together was "very difficult." It was not an easy or simple situation. This was no small thing. In other parts of the Soviet Bloc, this same situation had destroyed churches, yet, in Tallinn, the believers stuck with it. They purposed to work together for the sake of the Kingdom of God here on earth, and the Lord apparently blessed their one-Body efforts. Several of the people with whom I spoke credit that working together as the main reason for the revival. Had it not been for them working together, they are convinced the revival would never have happened.

Some people believe a third primary cause of the revival is the fact that people were diligently seeking the Lord. They wanted to be closer to Him, to know Him and be known by Him, so they regularly gathered together and prayed. They not only wanted to know Him, but they also wanted others to know Him.

Rein declared, "If we truly want to see revival, we must act like a farmer who is awaiting harvest." They sowed the seeds of prayer, asking God to cleanse their own hearts and lives and to open the hearts of the people to the gospel. The Lord apparently acted on those prayers. He heard them and answered.

Several people I interviewed told me emphatically that they didn't go into this hoping to see miracles. No, they just wanted to know the Lord more intimately and to have others know Him that way, too. From my research, it looked to me like they were seeking God and stumbled across the power of God. Some would call it an accident. I, on the other hand, don't think it was accidental at all. It clearly happened as a result of them seeking Him.

Another factor that likely helped cause the revival was the evangelistic outreach. Pastor Oskar Olvik set out to win others, especially young people, to Christ. He wanted to see the thousands of people from all across the city of Tallinn in heaven someday. So he planned a creative approach to win souls. And it worked. Actually, because Olvik died in 1977, here on earth he never realized that it worked far beyond what he had imagined. I'm pretty sure that Pastor Olvik never envisioned hundreds of new churches resulting from his little evangelistic efforts. That wasn't his goal, yet it was the ultimate outcome. By the time it was all done, thousands and thousands of people had been rescued from eternal separation from God. It happened because one man responded to the prompting of the Holy Spirit not to remain complacent and stagnant. Under the Communist regime, he risked everything to evangelize. I'm pretty sure that, if Olvik were alive here on earth today, he would say that his efforts more than paid off.

A fifth reason that some believe the revival happened is because of the location. Estonia was the farthest western Soviet country. It is very near to Finland. Because of this, there is relatively easy access to the West. If something significant happened in Estonia, it quickly would be acknowledged in the western media. This resulted in the Communists allowing some measure of freedom in Tallinn, as this would offer the perception that there was religious freedom throughout the entire Soviet Union. This was, of course, only a mask — a tactic to deceive the rest of the world — but one the Soviets hoped would work. Perhaps in their effort to portray religious freedom, they let it go too far.

Another reason that some people think the revival happened in Tallinn, is that in a society that declares there is no God, perhaps something more than spoken words is necessary. Words are vital, but a clear demonstration of God's power will certainly get people's attention. Like the parting of the Red Sea or the miracles in the book of Acts, there seem to be times when God displays His power in more tangible and evident ways. It appears that the revival in Tallinn was one of those.

Some people might suggest that the welcoming of the Russians may have been a catalyst for the revival. There can be no doubt that willingly including the much-hated Russians was a godly action. After all, Jesus did say: "Love your enemies and pray for those who persecute you" (Matthew 5:44). It seems to me that this is exactly what the folks at Oleviste did. So did God bless them because of their actions? Was He so pleased with such love and prayers that He blessed them far beyond their expectations? It is certainly possible, but, of course, we don't know for sure.

Finally — and this was inferred by a few different people, but never stated directly — revivals, both in Scripture and in history in general, usually have some sort of leader, or even several leaders. Most of the time there is a person, or persons, with a true passion and calling and a heart for God. In Tallinn there were a few such leaders. Pastor Oskar Olvik, the man who began the Effataa Choir outreach, got the ball rolling. His vision and willingness to step out helped set the stage for the revival. Another man whose name I heard several times as I researched, Jaanus Karner, began the contemporary music meetings at the Methodist Church in Tallinn. Those meetings were foundational for what happened later at Oleviste. And, of course, there was also Rein Uuemõis. When I interviewed him about his remembrances for this book, he was over eighty years old. The end of the revival was more than thirty years in the past. He had shared the story with me two years before, and I heard the intensity in his voice then. Now, two years later, my perception was that he was even *more* passionate about God. Many with whom I spoke told of the influence his spiritual walk had on their own lives. Over and over, I heard stories of how Rein's life had affected others. That heart and passion for God was a major motivating force in the revival. Without Rein, or at least someone like him, it is very unlikely that the revival would have happened.

This side of heaven, we probably will never know exactly why the revival occurred. All of these reasons could have played into it. Perhaps even other factors were involved, also. Regardless, we do know that God worked in amazing ways and, in doing so, drew tens of thousands of people closer to Himself.

Something profound and interesting happened more than two decades before the start of the revival. At the end of World War II, there was a Pentecostal prayer meeting in Tallinn. During one of those meetings, a woman shared what she believed was a prophetic word, a fore-telling of what God would do. She said that there would come a revival at Oleviste Church, and it would come through young people. At the time, Oleviste sat vacant and dilapidated, an empty shell. It was a vivid reminder of the spiritual heritage of Tallinn, but also a symbol of what the despised Communist occupation had done.

Those who heard what the woman had shared thought the idea absurd. How could there be a revival in an ancient cathedral that was empty and decaying? The very thought of it was ridiculous. The woman continued by saying that the revival would go on, but then firemen would come and put the fire out. Although most people likely thought the woman was just crazy, at least one person who was at that meeting never forgot what she said.

It was years later that the revival did indeed occur. It happened just as the woman had predicted, and it began with the young people. Eventually, though, the firemen came and put the fire out.

For a while, the Communists looked the other way while Oleviste began their small evangelistic services. Likely, they believed they could keep things under control while showing the world that the Soviets were openly allowing religious freedom. As the services grew, though, I am sure the authorities began to wonder whether this was such a good idea. When as many as fifteen hundred people from all across the Soviet Union attended each service, there must have been some very serious concern among the government officials. In the fall of 1980, the authorities decreed that the services could no longer be translated into Russian or any other language. Only the Estonian language could be spoken in the services.

Not long before this event, the secret police had begun to turn up the heat. The services at Oleviste were clearly getting out of hand. Each second and fourth Friday evening and Saturday morning, the train station in Tallinn was packed with people coming to Oleviste. Those who arrived on Friday night often slept overnight on the floor of the train station. Although in our prosperous society today, most of us might think it preposterous even to *consider* sleeping on the floor of a train station, these people did not. They were not twenty-first century Americans. This was the late 1970s, and these folks lived in Communist Russia. They were poor. They had nowhere else to go. For them it was no big deal. Many were sick and hungry, but it made no difference. They had to sleep, and the floor was available. They simply took advantage of the convenient and free lodging. For the local authorities, though, it was a travesty.

It wasn't only the train station, though. Even the airport was crowded with people coming to visit Oleviste Church. Those who came from far away, and who had the economic means, traveled by plane. Every other weekend saw an increase in travel to and from Tallinn.

I was told that sometimes so many Russians crowded around the church that they blocked traffic in the street. There were times when the police went to the airport, railway station, and even to the church, and sent people back home before they had a chance to get into the church building. The authorities were clearly unhappy with what was happening and were starting to push back in a more determined way.

Further, during the summer of 1980, the Soviet Union hosted the Olympic Games. Most Americans don't recall those competitions, because the United States and other western nations boycotted them due to the Soviet involvement in the war in Afghanistan. Even those of us who are old enough to remember have little or no recollection of what happened. Yet there was an interesting twist that plays into the Oleviste story. You see, all of the Olympic competitions were held in Moscow, except one. The yachting event could not be held in the Soviet capitol city because of the lack of a large body of water. Instead, that event was hosted in Tallinn, Estonia.

Because of this, international visitors swarmed into the city. Those visitors were not just confined to the official yachting area, though. They also made their way to historic Old Town Tallinn, where Oleviste Church was, and still is, a prominent landmark. As this happened, there were the inevitable questions about the crowds at Oleviste, the sickly people sleeping on the floor of the train station, the difficulty in finding flights on certain weekends. All of this caused the higher-ups to put immense pressure on the local officials to take care of this embarrassing mess.

Clean up the mess they did. Valdur Timusk, head of the secret police in Tallinn, threatened Rein Uuemõis and others with larger fines and even imprisonment. They turned up the heat. Although there had been arrests and threats all along, those things suddenly escalated and became more intense. The Communists promised to close the church completely and take away the rights of the pastors to minister anywhere else if the services continued to offer translation. Only the native language — Estonian — could be used. Any more translating, and the government would be forced to take even more serious action.

Ülo Meriloo had become the pastor of Oleviste after Oskar Olvik passed away. During this period, Meriloo was frequently called to the secret police headquarters next door to answer questions. He took most of the pressure so others wouldn't have quite so much. Some say it was his diplomatic efforts that delayed the ultimate end of the revival.

Eventually, though, the Communists had their way. Their decree that the services could no longer be translated into Russian meant an end to the Russians coming. Only a miniscule percentage of those visitors could understand any Estonian at all. This meant that anything spoken would no longer be comprehended, so they stopped coming. It was a sad time for those at Oleviste, not to mention throughout the Soviet Union.

Today, Rein clearly says that stopping was a mistake. He admits that he never should have agreed to cease the translations. He rues the fact that, as one of the elders of the church, he signed the document agreeing to stop the translations. He is sorry that he bowed to the pressure, but since his friends and fellow believers were being threatened, I don't know that he had many options. I'm pretty sure that, given the same circumstances, I likely would have made the same decision.

For all practical purposes, the revival then ended. They still held services, but it wasn't the same. Far fewer people came. The salvations and healings were not nearly as numerous as they had been. Eventually, it just stopped altogether. The firemen had done their job. They had come in and put out the fire. †

Chapter 6

Lessons Learned

Since the time I first began sharing this story with Christians in America, people have asked me, "What did you learn from what you heard there?" Actually, there were plenty of amazing lessons I encountered. Some of these I already knew, but they were strongly reinforced as the story unfolded through research and interviews. As a teacher in the Body of Christ, I would be remiss if I didn't share with you the lessons that I think are the most significant.

- **God doesn't need ideal circumstances to do His work.** God did some amazing, miraculous things during the revival. Thousands of people were born-again. Thousands more were physically healed. At the same time, not everything was rosy and pretty. In fact, sometimes things got rough.

Each of the key leaders in the revival was arrested at some point, most more than once. At various times, Pastor Oskar Olvik, Rein Uuemõis, Ülo Niinemägi, and even Arnold Turkin (the maintenance man at the church) were all nabbed by the secret police, interrogated, and threatened. Although most people are still reluctant to talk about their interactions with those government agents, I did hear stories of hefty fines, homes being searched, and various possessions confiscated.

A few different eyewitnesses told me about agents of the secret police regularly visiting the services. Sometimes they even took photos. I already mentioned the surveillance camera mounted on the building next door and pointed at Oleviste Church. The Communist authorities were definitely keeping an eye on what was happening at the church.

When Communism fell and Estonia regained freedom, the building that was next door to Oleviste Church — the secret police headquarters — was abandoned. Those who first entered the building after it was vacated found an area that was horrific to even write about. It was a room where the floor opened downward, like trap doors. Beneath that floor was a gruesome machine that apparently had seen plenty of use through the years. One eyewitness referred to it as a giant meat grinder. It was a means of disposing of people. There were those who went into the secret police headquarters and were never heard from again. They went down into that grisly machine, and their ground-up remains were washed into the sewer. All that to say that the threats of the government were not idle words. These guys were serious. When they spoke, people listened.

Jesus' original disciples faced threats and persecution, yet they apparently knew and understood something that we generally don't today. Peter and John were brought before the rulers and elders and scribes in Jerusalem. Those leaders — basically the same group that spearheaded the arrest and crucifixion of Jesus — told the disciples to stop speaking in the name of Jesus, but Peter and John refused. Afterward the disciples prayed: "And now, Lord, look upon their threats and grant to your servants to continue to speak your word with all boldness, while you stretch out your hand to heal, and signs and wonders are performed through the name of your holy servant Jesus" (Acts 4:29-30).

I find this prayer fascinating. They didn't ask to be protected. They didn't ask for God to hide them from their enemies. They didn't even pray for the death or destruction of their foes. No, instead, these guys requested boldness. They wanted the Lord to give them strength to speak fearlessly and for God's work to continue unabated, even while they were being persecuted.

Similarly, the leaders in Tallinn heard the threats of the government officials, but they paid little heed to them. Instead, they continued to press forward in the work to which God had called them.

Personally, I find comfort in Hebrews 11:32-34: "And what more shall I say? For time would fail me to tell of Gideon, Barak, Samson, Jephthah, of David and Samuel and the prophets — who through faith conquered kingdoms, enforced justice, obtained promises, stopped the mouths of lions, quenched the power of fire, escaped the edge of the sword, were made strong out of weakness, became mighty in war, put foreign armies to flight." From our human perspective, these don't seem to be ideal circumstances. Lions, wars, swords — those are things I would just as soon avoid. Such things sound menacing to me, yet God had His way in spite of ominous conditions. You see, the truth is that God doesn't need ideal circumstances to do His work.

Actually, after writing that last statement, I wonder if I should qualify it a bit. Honestly, the Lord *always* works in ideal situations. It's just that our notion of ideal is not the same as God's. We want everything pretty and nice. Low stress. Happy endings. Warm fuzzies all around. Apparently, God's definition of "ideal" doesn't always, or even *usually*, look like that.

When Rein was just nine years old, his father was taken away to Siberia. He was gone for three and a half years. The living conditions in Siberia were unspeakable. Those who guarded the prisoners had little concern about whether those prisoners lived or died. If they were worked to death or frozen to death, so be it. Being subjected to such conditions can change one's appearance dramatically. When Rein's father returned, the family barely recognized him. He, in turn, scarcely knew his children because they had grown and changed so much. However, when his father returned, he came back, as Rein phrases it, as a "wholehearted believer." Something had changed during his incarceration in Siberia. God had used that horrendous and grueling ordeal to draw Rein's dad closer to Himself.

The Lord does not need to have ideal circumstances to do His work. He can cause His plans and purposes to be realized, in spite of dark and difficult times. Sometimes that can happen specifically *because* of those dark and difficult times.

Today, in our country, there is a seemingly ever-increasing anti-Christian sentiment — and in some cases even open hostility toward Christians — in both the society and the government. Christian-bashing, in many ways, is in vogue. Statements — made by media personalities or government officials about Christians and the Christian faith — would never be tolerated if such statements were made about Muslims or Hindus, but Christians are open targets.

Some people would say that the Lord can't work in such circumstances, yet history would repeatedly deny such an idea. In the book of Acts, the Church grew initially by thousands at a time, under extreme persecution. Today, the nation with the most believers is China. Realistic estimates range to more than 200,000,000 Christians in that anti-God, Communistic society.

Someone recently sent me a profound quote. In the movie, *Harry Potter and the Goblet of Fire*, Albus Dumbledore says, "Dark and difficult times lie ahead. Soon we must all face the choice between what is right and what is easy." What an apt description of our society today. Living as a true believer in Christ is not necessarily easy in an anti-Christian society, but it is still the right thing to do, and God will strengthen you to make it reality, if you ask Him.

If you're waiting to do something until everything is perfect, you will be waiting far longer than necessary. Don't allow the anti-Christian bent of our culture to stop you from trusting His faithfulness and sovereignty. God is still ruling and reigning. Even in the midst of difficult times, He will ultimately prevail.

The revival in Tallinn reminds us that God does not need to have ideal circumstances to do His work. He can — and will — have His way regardless of who or what tries to stop Him.

▪ **Christian unity is paramount to God.**

When Rein Uuemõis first shared this astounding story with me, the thing he emphasized was the different churches working together. To Rein, this was not a side issue. It was definitely not a coincidence that the various Christian churches — with *very* different theological persuasions — were thrust together and forced to work in cooperation with one another. Although it was brought about by the Communists, it was, evidently, part of God's plan. He wants His people unified.

Toward the end of Jesus' visible earthly ministry, the religious leaders held a council because He had become too popular. They were trying to figure out what to do with Him. Caiaphas, the high priest, declared that it would be better "that one man should die for the people, not that the whole nation should perish" (John 11:50). In essence, he was saying, "Let's just get rid of this guy so that the rest of us won't suffer because of him." In Caiaphas' mind, that's apparently what he intended. Yet, Scripture declares that the idea of taking Jesus' life wasn't really Caiaphas' idea.

"He did not say this of his own accord, but being high priest that year he prophesied that Jesus would die for the nation" (John 11:51). But the biblical narrative does not stop there. Instead, it goes on to say, "and not for the nation only, *but also to gather into one the children of God who are scattered abroad*" (John 11:52, author's emphasis).

As Christians, we emphatically declare that Jesus' death reconciles us to God. Often, though, we miss the other part of the reconciliation: to one another. "To gather into one the children of God." There can be no doubt that unity of believers is a high priority for God.

In his letter to the church at Ephesus, the Apostle Paul talks about the division between Jews and Gentiles.

He then goes on to say that Jesus, through His atoning sacrifice, "has made us both one and has broken down in his flesh the dividing wall of hostility" (Ephesians 2:14). Jesus' death and resurrection indeed reconcile us to God, but those things also reconcile us to one another. We are one in Him.

One of the people mentioned to me repeatedly as being a key leader during the revival was Karl Reinaru. Karl was a Lutheran pastor. Bear in mind that Lutherans have very different beliefs on several major theological issues than, say, Baptists. So for someone of that theological persuasion to work alongside Baptists and others must have been extremely difficult. Some of their key doctrinal beliefs would necessarily need to be set aside for the sake of the overall kingdom work. And that is apparently what Karl Reinaru willingly did.

1 Corinthians 12:27 declares: "Now you are the body of Christ and individually members of it." All who profess Christ as Savior, regardless of their other theological leanings, are part and parcel of one body. We are not separate entities. We are one.

Think about it this way: how useful would your hand be if it was cut off from the rest of your body? Not much, right? That's the point of us being the body of Christ. We are, of course, connected to Him, but we are also connected to one another.

Through His death and resurrection, Jesus has made us to be one. We can rationalize our differences — denominational and otherwise — all day long, but it is clear from His Word that the Lord wants us to be unified in Him.

Rein became the next senior pastor of Oleviste after Ülo Meriloo. During his tenure, Rein eagerly helped organize all the pastors in Tallinn to meet together and pray. He pursued his dream of a presbytery of pastors in Tallinn that would oppose the darkness, and, in unity, draw the city toward the light of Christ. Rein had seen what true Christian unity could do, and he wanted more of it.

In light of the Oleviste story, I can't help but wonder about the *true potential* of the Church in America. What would happen if we willingly set aside the things that divide us and chose to walk together in love and unity? If we recognize that Jesus' death and resurrection are our only hope for salvation, why do we fight over our differences about end times? Are such things *really* that important? Especially in light of the fact that God's Word declares that part of the reason why Jesus came was "to gather into one the children of God."

The night before He went to the cross, Jesus prayed for you and me: "I do not ask for these only, but also for those who will believe in me through their word..." (John 17:20). If you understand those words, He is praying for us, even today. So what was it that Jesus was praying for? "That they may all be one, just as you, Father, are in me, and I in you..." (John 17:21a). He clearly and obviously wants us to be unified, wants us to be one in Him.

To God, Christian unity is paramount. At Oleviste Church, He openly demonstrated how potent unity really can be. Christian churches of various backgrounds willingly worked together and eventually saw God move in a mighty way. It may well have been the largest revival of the twentieth century, and it was a result of their working together.

The question for us today is, now that we know how vital Christian unity is and what impact it can have, what will we do? Will we continue as we have been, fiercely independent and refusing to work together with our brothers and sisters in Christ, or will we willingly allow the Lord to work in and through us, causing us to truly become one in Him?

▪ God is a rewarder of those who seek Him.

The leaders of the revival met regularly for prayer. They had a deep desire to gather frequently and pray. Sometimes they were together daily for prayer, and it wasn't simply a forced expression – "You had better do this, or else." No, they really wanted to pray.

Scripture says, "Whoever would draw near to God must believe that he exists and that he rewards those who seek him" (Hebrews 11:6). Clearly, God rewards those who seek Him. But what does it mean to seek the Lord?

I would suggest that, in large measure, seeking the Lord is a heart issue. After all, God spoke through the prophet Jeremiah with these words: "You will seek me and find me, when you seek me with all your heart. I will be found by you, declares the LORD" (Jeremiah 29:13-14).

An honest seeking of God requires a wholehearted pursuit. The Lord is apparently not interested in a halfway, lackadaisical attitude. It's full out or not at all.

Jesus quoted the prophet Isaiah: "This people honors me with their lips, but their heart is far from me" (Matthew 15:8). Lip service without the heart is obviously the wrong way, but there is a better way. The great reformer, Martin Luther, once said, "Grant that I may not pray with my mouth alone; help me that I may pray from the depths of my heart." Luther clearly nailed that one.

Rein recognized that God was not content with beautiful meetings, nice music, and great speeches. He wants people whose hearts are turned toward Him. He desires for us to seek Him wholeheartedly.

In Tallinn, the regular prayer meetings — and ultimately the revival itself — were an expression of hearts that were pursuing God. I heard from several of those involved early in the revival that they were seeking the Lord for more. They were not satisfied with their lives, and so they sought the Lord to move them forward in their walk of faith.

One pastor, Udo Veevo, started coming to meetings at Oleviste before the main time of revival began. He lived on Hiuma, an Estonian island in the Baltic Sea. At the time, he was actually not a full-time pastor. He was an engineer with the telephone company, but he saw the obvious fingerprints of God on the meetings at Oleviste. Unfortunately, it took far too long to cross over on the ferry and then drive to Tallinn. Instead, for several years, he purchased a plane ticket and flew there twice a month. If God was doing profound and even miraculous works there, Udo wanted to be a part of it. Udo Veevo is now deceased, but according to his wife and son, it cost him between 10%-20% of his salary to make those trips. Yet even today, his wife and son say it was money well-spent. Udo Veevo was wholeheartedly seeking the Lord, regardless of the cost. God was more important to him than money. I wonder how many in our society could say the same.

I thoroughly enjoyed hearing the stories of the Russians and others who came from hundreds, and even thousands, of miles away. Long train rides and flights brought those who were seeking God. They weren't willing to remain complacent. They had a deep desire to pursue the Lord. Both Rein Uuemõis and Ülo Niinemägi, now an associate pastor at Oleviste, say that the people involved had a "holy dissatisfaction." They wanted to know — and be known by — the God they read about in the Bible.

As I interviewed those who were there during the revival, the thing I heard over and over was that there was an intense hunger for God, and, therefore, an intense seeking of God. Clearly, the Lord honored that seeking. He rewards those who diligently seek Him.

• **Even in the midst of God's blessing, not everything is going to be perfect.**
It was nearly two years from the time I first asked,

before Rein agreed to allow me to write the story of the revival. Much of his reluctance was because, as he put it, "Americans like sensationalism." He wanted the whole story told, not just the happy parts. He didn't want people to think that everything was perfect during those years. Although they saw amazing blessings from God, many things happened that were not fun.

People who traveled to Oleviste from farther away often brought food with them into the services. The most common was a sandwich wrapped in newspaper. Unfortunately, those newspapers often ended up on the floor of the church. When I've gone to Major League Baseball games, I have always been amazed at the mess that is left when the game is done. Papers, cups, leftover food, scorecards... trash everywhere. What a mess! After talking with those involved in the meetings at Oleviste, I get the impression that such a baseball stadium scene might just be an accurate depiction of what the church looked like when the services were over. People may have been healed and born-again, but that didn't mean they weren't messy. This was simply a holdover from their Communist society. No one respected property. They didn't care if they made a mess. And it fell to the leaders at Oleviste to clean up that mess, picking up garbage, mopping floors, cleaning restrooms. Everything needed to be returned to pristine condition for the service the next morning. Yet even in the midst of this activity, there was a spirit of unity, love, and cooperation. Everyone – from Rein to the prayer warriors to the choir members to the church maintenance man,

Arnold Turkin – willingly pitched in and helped make the job easier.

God's blessings may be obvious, but that does not mean everything will be perfect. When the Israelites were going into the Promised Land, they still had battles to fight. Even though God had promised them the land as an inheritance, it was still necessary for them to engage in warfare — hand-to-hand combat — with enemies who didn't want them there. Jesus told the first disciples to go and preach the gospel, yet they were opposed at nearly every turn. Just because the Lord is involved in an activity — even though He is clearly and obviously blessing something — that does not mean there won't be problems, or even opposition. Someone recently said that like the sun shining while it's raining, sometimes contradictory things happen in life. It's true.

A case can be made that the Apostle Paul walked as closely with God and followed Him as wholeheartedly as anyone in the Bible. Yet even through his amazing spiritual journey, Paul frequently had problems. Whipped, beaten with rods, shipwrecked, a day and a night in the open sea, stoned and left for dead... these were not fun times. And everyone knows about Paul's "thorn in the flesh" (2 Corinthians 12:7). Such things seem contradictory to the blessing of God on someone's life.

Many of the leaders at Oleviste Church were arrested and threatened by the secret police. Pastor Olvik, who began the Effataa choir meetings, died at the end of 1977, just as the revival truly took off. He had supported the meetings right from the beginning, but the interrogations, threats, and constant pressure were just too much. Even the church's maintenance man was interrogated by the authorities This was a difficult time for those involved in the revival. At the same time, though, seeing souls saved and people healed month after month must have made it an exhilarating and uplifting time, as well. The sun was shining, but the rain continued to fall.

Today, Rein's son is very solid in his faith. In fact, he is even the head of the elders at Oleviste Church. The unfortunate truth, though, is that both of Rein's daughters are what he terms "not active Christians." For someone as zealous in faith as Rein, that must be a very deep wound. I have never experienced such a thing so I cannot relate, but I can imagine that the pain must be difficult.

The fact is that we live in a world filled with sin. Sometimes we will have difficulties, even while we are sharing in the blessings of God. Not everything is going to be perfect.

▪ God Answers When His People Cry Out to Him

One of the most profound lessons I learned at Oleviste happened before I even heard about the revival. I was there at the church to preach the first of three services that Sunday morning. As with many old cathedrals, the pulpit is high up on the front wall. The approach to this one is from directly behind it, a short walk up ten steps.

Ülo Niinemägi, an assistant pastor at the church, was to be my translator. He wanted me to see the pulpit beforehand, so, well before the first service began, he took me up the steps to check it out. However, as we started through the doorway to begin our ascent, he stopped me and said, "Later, when we go up these steps, stop on each step and pray for God's anointing."

I knew what he meant. It is something that has been a part of my ministry since day one. I know that if God doesn't do the work, all my words are useless. Unless the Lord works in and through His Word to bring life and inspiration to the hearers, my words, regardless of how eloquent they may be, will not have the full effect they should.

So, Ülo was telling me to pray that God's anointing would rest on me, and that the words would have their full effect in the minds and hearts of the people. I heard what he said and assured him that I would do that when we went up the steps later during the service.

When the time came for the sermon, though, I had forgotten his admonition. I was so focused on what I was about to say and how I was going to say it, that I neglected his encouragement to invite the Lord into the situation. In my usual take-charge, let's-go attitude, I was ready to bound up the stairs two at a time. But as we approached the doorway to ascend the stairs, he gently grabbed my arm and said, "Pray for God's anointing."

I knew he was right. So we slowly went up the steps, stopping on each one just long enough to entrust ourselves, our words, our hearts, and our minds into the hands of the Holy Spirit, that He might accomplish His plans and purposes that morning. When we reached the top, I wasn't the least bit anxious. I knew that God was in charge.

It wasn't until much later that I realized that Ülo had apparently learned that lesson during the revival. Pray. Without God's intervention, nothing of real significance is going to happen.

As I interviewed those involved in the Oleviste revival, one of the primary messages I heard over and over was that they prayed. They prayed often. They prayed together. They prayed alone. They did their best to, as 1 Thessalonians 5:17 says, "pray without ceasing." They cried out to God. They wanted Him to move in their own lives, in their church, in their city, in their nation, and throughout the Soviet Union. They prayed. And He, in turn, responded.

In the minds of those who were there, prayer was the undergirding for the entire phenomenon. Without exception, they believe that if they had not prayed, the revival would not have occurred. Even today, thirty years after the revival ended, they are all adamantly convinced that God answers when His people cry out to Him.

Jesus repeatedly talked about and demonstrated the priority of prayer.

- "And rising very early in the morning, while it was still dark, he departed and went out to a desolate place, and there he prayed" (Mark 1:35).

- "In these days he went out to the mountain to pray, and all night he continued in prayer to God" (Luke 6:12).
- "Now Jesus was praying in a certain place" (Luke 11:1).
- The entire seventeenth chapter of John's Gospel is a prayer Jesus prayed.
- "And going a little farther he fell on his face and prayed" (Matthew 26:39).

If the Son of God recognized the necessity of prayer in His earthly life, how much more should we?

Jim Cymbala, pastor of the renowned Brooklyn Tabernacle, made this observation in his book *Fresh Wind, Fresh Fire*:

> Satan's main strategy with God's people has always been to whisper, "Don't call, don't ask, don't depend on God to do great things. You'll get along fine if you just rely on your own cleverness and energy." The truth of the matter is that the devil is not terribly frightened of our human efforts and credentials. But he knows his kingdom will be damaged when we lift up our hearts to God.[1]

I think Cymbala has a good point. The people at Oleviste, though, apparently ignored the whispers of the enemy that would urge them away from prayer. They prayed... a lot.

In his book, *Spiritual Disciplines of the Christian Life*,

Donald Whitney made a powerful assertion:

> Often we do not pray because we doubt that any-
> thing will actually happen if we pray. Of course, we
> don't admit this publicly. But if we felt certain of
> visible results within sixty seconds of every prayer,
> there would be holes in the knees of every pair of
> Christian-owned pants in the world![2]

He's right. If we honestly took God at His Word, we would not need someone to prod us to spend time in prayer.

Yet, even if we acknowledge prayer as being important, it can still remain a mystery to us. It can be a conundrum, a puzzle that we can't seem to solve. We may not be willing to openly admit such things, but inside we still wonder.

Let's be completely honest for a moment. Does prayer really make any sense to you? Doesn't it seem outlandish, at best, to suggest that the God of the Universe — the One Who created everything there is, including you and me — would tie Himself to our prayers? Doesn't such a notion seem presumptuous, perhaps even bordering on blasphemy? After all, who do we think we are?

The truth of God's Word, though, tells us that it is true. The Most High Lord has, indeed, somehow connected Himself to our prayers. You cannot honestly read the Bible and deny that fact. When people pray, God moves. When people don't pray, God withholds His hand.

That's why the folks at Oleviste prayed regularly.

They followed the scriptural pattern and the scriptural mandate: "Continue steadfastly in prayer..." (Colossians 4:2). They prayed. Maybe we should, too.

- **Today's spiritual victories do not guarantee tomorrow's.**

Sunday morning, after I had preached at Oleviste Church the second time, a woman approached me and asked for prayer. Her husband had left her several years ago, and he was now on his third wife. She shared some of the resulting pain she had experienced, and she asked me to pray for her and, also, for her former husband. I prayed as she had requested.

It wasn't until later, as I interviewed those who were involved in the revival, that I realized that her husband had been one of the early leaders. He was involved in the prayer meetings with Rein and others, the very prayer meetings that were apparently the catalyst that sparked the revival. He had been there week after week. He had seen people born again. He had witnessed those who were physically impaired returned to health. He knew the saving and healing power of God, yet now he had abandoned it all.

Proverbs 4:23, says: "Above all else, guard your heart, for it is the wellspring of life." (NIV) Regardless of how spiritual you are, no matter whether you have witnessed firsthand true miracles from God, if you don't consistently guard your heart, you may very well end up in trouble. Today's spiritual victories do not guarantee tomorrow's.

If you read the Old Testament, there seems to be a recurring cycle. God works on behalf of His people. After awhile, though, they get complacent. They forget about the Lord. They walk away from the Source of their strength. In doing so, the inevitable happens: they are defeated in battle. Then they turn back to God, and the whole cycle starts over. As we read such sections of Scripture, it looks as though the Lord abandoned them when they were defeated. Truthfully, He did, but if you really understand the situation, it was only because they had first abandoned Him.

It's easy to do. It's not at all difficult to become self-reliant. It is a seemingly natural human response — because of our fallenness — to abandon God and begin to think we can make it without Him. Slowly — even imperceptibly — our faith can grow cold. If not cold, then perhaps lukewarm. Honestly, that may be even worse.

Please recognize that God will not leave us or forsake us, but we certainly have the ability to walk away from Him. Of course, we would generally not do that intentionally. No one sets out to suddenly do an about-face in their walk with God. We can, though, make little choices each day that take us down a path that ultimately leaves the Lord behind.

Although this amazing revival began in Estonia, that nation shows little evidence of the revival today. A recent

BBC article suggests that Estonia is the least religious nation in the world. Fewer than 20% say that any religion plays a role at all in their lives. What a sad — and sobering — statistic.

Just because you've seen the Lord move in powerful and miraculous ways, don't begin to think that you're something special. Don't get the idea that you can coast and ignore all that got you to that point. Today's spiritual victories do not guarantee tomorrow's.

————————————————————◦•◦●●◦●●◦◦————————————————————

- **God is ruling and reigning, regardless of how things appear.**

In 1944, when the Russians returned to Estonia, Rein's grandmother, a determined woman, decided that the family should leave the country. She declared that the next morning they would pack all their belongings, go to Läänemaa (the westernmost province of mainland Estonia) to hide from the war, and then go to sea from there. Rein and his brother, Haljand, slept in the hayloft that night. The next morning they were awakened by a strange sound. On the road a long column of Russian tanks were rolling in. That meant an end to their plans. It was not, however, an end to God's plans. Despite the way things looked — it *appeared* as though the Communists had foiled the family's plans — today Rein recognizes that the Lord kept him in Estonia for a reason.

During the height of the revival, Rein was, once

again, summoned to the secret police headquarters. He was questioned about the healings that were taking place at the church. Rein had to explain to the government officials what was going on. When he did, though, the government agents declared there was no healing. There couldn't be. If there is no such thing as God, how could He be healing people? It was all just a fantasy.

The ironic part was that, in sharp contrast to their claims, the front of Mary Chapel was filled with canes, walkers, crutches, even eye-glasses, of people who had been healed. Those abandoned devices were a strong testimony that the Lord did indeed exist, and that He was indeed healing people. This scene reminds me of a cartoon I saw years ago. A man was standing with his eyes closed and his fingers plugging his ears. The caption read, "Don't confuse me with the facts, my mind is made up."

"The fool says in his heart, 'There is no God'" (Psalm 14:1; 53:1). In the midst of clear and obvious evidence, the Communists still insisted that God did not exist. How foolish.

When they effectively shut down the revival, it appeared they had won. Take careful note that we must never allow ourselves to be fooled by appearances. It was less than a decade later that the iron curtain fell, and the Communists were no longer in power. They hadn't really won at all. It may have looked like they won the victory in that minor little skirmish, but there can be no doubt that the Lord is the ultimate Victor.

In 1971, Apollo 15 astronaut, James Irwin, became

the eighth man to walk on the moon. Ten years later, in 1981, Irwin visited Oleviste Church. The Communists tried to persuade him not to speak at the church. They even offered him money to change his plans. They didn't want a famous American astronaut giving credibility to a religious organization. Irwin went to Oleviste anyway. As he spoke to the congregation, he told them that the God who walks on earth is far more important than a man who walks on the moon. He spoke of many miracles that God had done in his own life. The speech he gave there was copied numerous times over and secretly distributed throughout the Soviet Union.

In the final analysis, God will have His way. Moses said it plainly, "Know therefore today, and lay it to your heart, that the LORD is God in heaven above and on the earth beneath; there is no other" (Deuteronomy 4:39). Despite dictators, evil despots, mean bosses, backbiting coworkers, or any other inconvenience here and now, God is still God. He is in charge, and He will, ultimately, have His way.

• God seems to prize patience.

Time seems to be a major factor in our lives. Hurry up and get somewhere. Wait for that person. Don't miss this appointment. Be sure you meet that rapidly-approaching deadline. Go fast. Finish quickly. Don't be late. It can feel overwhelming. Yet God exists outside of time. He does not have the same constraints that encumber us. The Almighty views time from a *very* different perspective. "For a thousand years in your sight are but as yesterday when it is past, or as a watch in the night" (Psalm 90:4).

Enno Tuulik, one of the people who was involved early in the leadership of the revival, said, "It would be wrong to say that it suddenly just burst forth." He is definitely correct about that. There were years of behind-the-scenes work that occurred.

The Communists forced the various churches to work together beginning in 1950. The regular and consistent prayer meetings began in the early 1970s. The Effataa Choir Evenings started in 1969. Yet the major part of the revival, when the Russians began coming, didn't break out until 1977. There seems to be a lot of wasted time in there. Nothing much was happening. Just waiting.

Well, that's not completely accurate. There wasn't really any "wasted" time at all. Instead, there was plenty of time for lots of prayer and for God moving the right people into the right places. The preparations were made and foundations were carefully laid. The spiritual undergirding was taking place. All of those things were essential preliminaries to the actual revival itself. In fact, I would say that without the waiting, the prayer, the planning — the spiritual groundwork — none of the outward and obvious manifestations — the salvations and other miracles — would have occurred.

I don't know all the specific reasons, but I do know that God seems to prize patience. From the Lord's perspective, learning to be patient is vital. It certainly appears to be far more important than we generally think it should be. Patience is something we usually talk about as a positive virtue, but it is too frequently lacking in our lives. At the same time, God obviously seems to value patience highly.

In the book of Revelation, three different churches — Ephesus, Thyatira, and Philadelphia — are all commended for their "patient endurance." If you know the context, you know there weren't many commendations being handed out in that section of Scripture. There were plenty of critiques, but not much in the way of accolades. Clearly, though, the Lord was pleased with their patient endurance. In God's sight, patience is a good thing. A really good thing.

James says: "Be patient, therefore, brothers, until the coming of the Lord. See how the farmer waits for the precious fruit of the earth, being patient about it, until it receives the early and the late rains. You also, be patient" (James 5:7-8). The Bible repeatedly tells us to have patience. Like the old song for kids says, "Have patience, don't be in such a hurry."

Let me try to make this practical. If we really want to know God and to see His kingdom having the full effect it should have here on earth, then patience is a necessity. We need to learn to be still and know that He is God (Psalm 46:10). We must recognize that it is through faith and patience that we inherit the promises of God (Hebrews 6:12). In the Old Testament, David reminds us that it was when he had *waited patiently* for the Lord that God inclined His ear toward David and heard his cry for help (Psalm 40:1).

How long was it from the time that David was anointed as king that he actually became the King of Israel? Most scholars put that time frame at more than a decade. What about the Apostle Paul? How long was it from the time that God rescued his soul until he began to preach to the Gentiles? Again, many long years.

I could go on, but I hope you get the point. God is not generally in a hurry. We are, but not Him. If seeing God's will fulfilled in our lives means that we must wait for years, maybe even decades — praying and laying spiritual foundations — then so be it.

He wants us to seek Him, but sometimes we have to seek for a long time. The folks in Tallinn learned the lesson well. God seems to prize patience.

- **God works through His people.**

Sunday morning, August 7, 2011, I had the privilege of preaching a second time at Oleviste Church. My sermon that morning was entitled, "God Wants to Work Through You." My premise was that God rarely works independently apart from His people. My scriptural basis was that we are the Body of Christ, based on 1 Corinthians 12:27.

One of the illustrations I used that day was the feeding of the 5,000. The story is one of the few that is found in all four gospels. We usually refer to it as "Jesus Feeding the 5,000," but I think that's a wrong title. Do you remember what He said to His disciples? "You give them something to eat" (Matthew 14:16; Mark 6:37; Luke 9:13). Jesus didn't do the work Himself. He turned that work over to His disciples. Of course, Jesus could have done it on His own, but He didn't. He got them involved in the ministry work.

That's just His way. He could do everything far better without us, but He allows us to be a part of what He is doing.

God works through His people... and those people don't need to be the paid professional church workers. At the time of the revival, Rein was an engineer. According to everyone with whom I spoke, he was apparently a really good engineer, one who was highly respected. He was not a pastor until more than a decade after the revival ended. The Lord worked then — and still does today — through normal, everyday folks like you and me.

"To each is given the manifestation of the Spirit for the common good" (1 Corinthians 12:7). Each of us has a specific role to play. Regardless of our level of intelligence, academic achievements, oratory skills, athletic abilities, management capabilities, good looks — or lack of any of these — the Lord will still work in and through us to accomplish His plans and purposes.

God also doesn't need a lot of people in order for His plans to be fulfilled. The Old Testament story of Gideon — he and his 300 men were victorious over the invading hoard of 135,000 — is a tremendous testimony to this truth. Actually, a few folks who make themselves available to the Lord is more than enough. The prayer meetings at Oleviste began with only a few people. Until the revival truly began in earnest, there were not more than a few dozen people praying for an outpouring.

The number of people with whom I spoke, and their varying roles in the revival, and their lives now, are also a clear testimony to the truth that God works through His people. Fishermen. Tax collectors. Engineers like Rein Uuemõis. Architects. Students. Stay-at-home moms. Just ordinary folks like you and me.

- **Not everyone is going to like it when God does something new.**
The revival services were held three times a month at Oleviste Church: the second and fourth Saturday evenings and the second Sunday evening. From late in 1977 until late in 1980, the church was packed to the brim for those services. It was standing room only nearly every single time. The aspect that I found odd, though, is that relatively few of the Sunday morning attenders were at those special services. According to the people with whom I spoke, fully two-thirds of the people who regularly attended on Sunday mornings had nothing to do with the revival. Either they simply did not participate or they were openly against it.

Honestly, throughout the entire time, the Sunday morning services remained nearly unchanged. The people there completely missed what God did, because it was new and different, out of the ordinary, even strange.

The truth is that God doesn't always do everything the same way. Just a quick look at creation should be enough to convince us of that. The nearly infinite variety of plants and animals ought to make it obvious that the Lord is boundlessly creative and doesn't always do everything the same way.

Take a look at Jesus' life. Sometimes when He healed a blind person He simply touched the person's eyes (Matthew 9:27-30, for example). Other times He spoke the Word and the person could see (Luke 18:35-42, for example). At least once, Jesus spit on the ground and made mud that He put on a blind man's eyes (John 9:1-6), and another time He apparently just spit directly on the person's eyes (Mark 8:22-25). It is clear that the Lord does not always do things the same way all the time.

Why then, do we often insist that He should? When something changes, why do we have a tendency to get upset? Why is it so hard for us to accept change?

Those of us who are in leadership roles should recognize that there will be opposition. When we sense a change in how we should approach ministry situations, there will be those who will oppose the change. Both Jesus and the Apostle Paul experienced the same thing. They were both following the Father's directives, yet each of them experienced opposition at nearly every turn.

Not everyone is going to like it when God does something new. The revival leaders at Oleviste recognized this. They continued to pray for the fellow believers who opposed what was going on, but they didn't allow those people to stop what God was doing.

My pastor once told me something that has helped me immensely in this regard. He said, "There are no monuments to critics." Don't worry about the naysayers. They will always be there. As leaders, we need to keep following where the Lord leads. Not everyone is going to like it when God does something new. And that's okay.

· Sometimes God demonstrates His power in ways beyond the usual.

As I heard the stories and read the testimonies of people who had been physically healed at Oleviste Church, I had to wonder, *Why?* Why did God do this supernatural thing in a place like Tallinn, Estonia? Why not everywhere, all the time?

We did, of course, explore this question earlier. Why the revival happened is a topic that nearly everyone who was there has an opinion about. But I want to look at it from a different perspective for a few moments, and give you my thoughts as a teacher in the Body of Christ.

Most Christians are familiar with the story of Jesus healing the paralytic man. Some of his friends lowered him through a roof to get him into the crowded room where Jesus was ministering. The story is told in three of the four Gospels. Luke's rendition, though, gives an interesting detail.

"And the power of the Lord was with him to heal" (Luke 5:17b). Other manuscripts read, "was present to heal them." Either way, the wording gives clear indication that this was beyond the usual. After all, if this was the norm, why declare that the power of the Lord was there? If this was everyday stuff, there would be no need for such phrasing. If the Lord's power was always present to heal, these words are redundant. Yet the words are there, telling us that something was different. This was beyond normal.

Apparently, sometimes in some places, God grants a dimension of His power that transcends the usual. Why did it happen this day in the life of Jesus and the people there? We don't know. Scripture doesn't tell us the answer to that question. It could be that people were praying behind the scenes. It could be a faith-filled expectancy on the part of the man's friends, a God-gift of supernaturally imparted faith. Whatever the reason, we know that the power of the Lord was there in a stronger than normal way.

Jonathan Edwards, the man who was at the forefront of what is known as the Great Awakening here in America, apparently witnessed a similar demonstration of the Holy Spirit's power at a specific time and place. He described it this way, "And then it was, in the latter part of

December, that the Spirit of God began extraordinarily to set it, and wonderfully to work amongst us. There were, very suddenly, one after another, five or six persons who were to all appearance savingly converted, and some of them in a very remarkable manner."[3] Edwards recognized that something out of the ordinary was happening.

It seems to me that a similar occurrence happened at Oleviste Church. Somehow, for a period of time, God demonstrated His power in ways beyond the norm. Things that don't usually happen, did happen in Tallinn.

We do know that God is not capricious. He doesn't just do things on a whim. The Lord is steady, constant, immovable. So regardless of why He sometimes demonstrates His power in stronger ways than He does in general, there is a reason. It is not because He is fickle. Somewhere beneath the surface, there is a purpose for the things He does. We may not always see His rationale, but it is there nonetheless.

At Oleviste Church, thousands upon thousands of people were healed. Certainly there were some minor healings that could even be explained in the natural realm. But so many major healings happened over a period of years, that there can be only one explanation: God was at work in ways that transcended the normal routine of life. For reasons that perhaps only He knows, the Lord reached down and physically changed people's bodies. Sicknesses and diseases were sent packing because God's power was made manifest in that place.

I don't know why — and likely none of us will ever

fully know why this side of eternity — but for some reason the Lord sometimes demonstrates His power in ways beyond the usual. Who knows? Perhaps He will do it again through you or me.

━━━━━━━━━━●●●●●●● ◄━━━━

▪ No matter how great the obstacles, God is greater.

Earlier I mentioned the steeple on Oleviste Church. At more than 400 feet tall, it was the highest point in Tallinn in the 1950s and '60s. No wonder, then, that the Communists decided to use it for their own purposes. It was the perfect location for the Soviets' plans. Electronic equipment was installed to block radio transmissions coming from the western world. Such a tall tower so close to the shore could be used effectively to impede those unwanted signals coming into Estonia. The steeple was also fitted with a transmitter necessary to send government messages to the higher-ups in Moscow. The Communists couldn't have asked for a better location. They didn't need to build it themselves. It was already in place when they took over. That church tower was perfect for their use.

It is ironic that right beneath that structure where anti-Soviet messages were blocked and pro-Soviet messages were transmitted, the Lord brought about one of the most amazing revivals in the history of the Church. The Communists thought they had found the perfect location for their plans, but God's plans immediately below were far more consequential. In the end, the Communist government was toppled, but hundreds of churches and thousands upon thousands of believers remain to this day as a result of the revival that happened right below that steeple.

Scripture is clear. No matter how great the obstacles, God is greater. John's first letter in the New Testament reminds us: "He who is in you is greater than he who is in the world" (1 John 4:4). The Apostle Paul declares: "If God is for us, who can be against us?" (Romans 8:31). Even the Old Testament psalmist assures us: "The LORD is on my side; I will not fear. What can man do to me?" (Psalm 118:6).

Personally, I love how blatantly the Lord displayed His might in Tallinn. The revival didn't happen across town from the tower that the Communists were utilizing. It didn't even occur down the road from it. No, God displayed His power right beneath that tower. It was as though He was trying to demonstrate that He was clearly mightier than the Communists.

I wrote this in a book some time ago, and I'm not sure exactly where it came from, but it bears repeating: "God is the unknown variable in any equation in your life, and the reason we think something won't work is because we don't realize how big that variable is." No matter how great the obstacles, God is greater. Always. †

Epilogue

Not long ago I read the testimony of a police detective. He said he came to faith in Christ after reading the four gospels. His explanation, though, was not at all what I expected. He said it was not because all four biblical accounts of Jesus' life lined up perfectly. In fact, it was because of the differences, the details that don't all seem to dovetail, that he was convinced.

The detective said that in police work, if there are

multiple witnesses, and all of their testimonies are exactly the same, it is generally because they are lying. They collaborated, conspired together beforehand on their statements, so they would all be the same. Without such collaboration, there are always differences, details that aren't precisely the same. Why? Because people remember different things, and they can even recall the same things somewhat differently. Their personalities and upbringing cause them to see things from different perspectives. What is vital to one person is insignificant to another. Testimonies of various eyewitnesses will almost never coincide exactly. That's why he believed the gospels. They weren't rehearsed ahead of time. There are some differences — not contradictions, but honest differences — in their stories that, from a detective's perspective, makes them more believable.

I am fairly certain that no one who was at Oleviste Church during the 1970s will be one-hundred percent satisfied with this book. I interviewed many people who saw things from very different perspectives. Except for a couple of "legend stories" — ones that have been told and retold so often that now everyone remembers them pretty much the same way — the recollections I heard varied greatly. None of them were contradictory, but certainly not all the details aligned perfectly. There were some variations.[1] Yet, for me as a researcher, I found that this offered credibility. It really did happen. There may not be complete agreement on all the minutiae, but the fact that God moved in powerful ways, bringing salvation to untold thousands and physical healing to thousands more, is clear and obvious to all.

I find it astounding that, in an era of unprecedented communication breakthroughs, the story of this revival was still somehow suppressed. Very few people in the West have ever heard even an inkling of this remarkable account. Because of this, I can't help but wonder what other amazing stories about God's work we have not been privy to. What is the *true* story of the Church in China, for example? Or what about the believers in the Middle East? What is their real story? Such stories may be every bit as big — maybe more so — than what you have just read.

The Holy Spirit is still alive and active on planet Earth. He is still bringing conviction to sinners and drawing people into a relationship with the Father through Jesus' atoning work on Calvary. He is still intervening in the lives and situations of His people around the world. He is still moving powerfully in and through His Church.

His intervention may not always appear quite as miraculous as the work in Tallinn, Estonia. Nevertheless, He is at work in His own miraculous way. The truth is that He is at work in your life, today.

I challenge you to regularly remember the lessons from Oleviste.

- *God doesn't need ideal circumstances to do His work.* He can accomplish His plans and purposes, regardless of the circumstances.
- *Christian unity is paramount to God.* If we, the

Church, were truly united, there would be no stopping us.

- *God is a rewarder of those who seek Him.* So seek Him.

- *Even in the midst of God's blessing, not everything is going to be perfect.* We will have problems and difficulties in this life.

- *God answers when His people cry out to Him.* So pray. And then pray some more.

- *Today's spiritual victories do not guarantee tomorrow's.* Keep your heart turned toward God. Always.

- *God is ruling and reigning, regardless of how things appear.* Don't be fooled by appearances; they can be deceptive.

- *God seems to prize patience.* Unlike our preference, God wants us to learn to be patient, and He is seemingly not in a hurry.

- *God works through His people.* Here on earth, He rarely works independently, apart from His people.

- *Not everyone is going to like it when God does something new.* There will always be those who oppose.

- *Sometimes God demonstrates His power in ways beyond the usual.* He did it for a paralytic man in the Bible; He did it at Oleviste Church, and He could do it again.

- *No matter how great the obstacles, God is greater.* He is far greater than any obstacle we will ever encounter.

No matter what happens in the natural realm, we can hang on to these scripturally-based lessons. According to God's Word, they are true. He emphasized them once again at Oleviste Church in Tallinn, Estonia. He will also demonstrate them in your life, here and now. The only question is whether you will let Him.

I pray that you will. †

Notes

Chapter 1
1. Jimmy Owens, "If My People Will Pray," ©1973 Bud John Songs, Inc.
2. John 4:10
3. John 4:14

Chapter 2
1. Toomas Vendelin, *Tallinn*, Pixelmeister OÜ, ©2005 Toomas Vendelin.
2. See also Acts 19:18

Chapter 3

1. Much of the information in this section is from an excellent documentary, *The Singing Revolution,* by James and Maureen Tusty, ©2008 Sky Films Inc. Art and Design and ©2008 New Video Group, Inc.

Chapter 4

1. It should be noted that I have tried to be conservative with the numbers used in this book. I would rather err on the side of being too low than to speak "evang-elastically." For example, official numbers that were given for two key events —the very first combined service at Oleviste and the Billy Graham service in 1984 —were 3000 and 4000 people respectively. Those services were counted and recorded. The revival services had no such records. The highest estimate I heard was 1500 people at a service. But I also heard that every seat was filled and people stood and sat in the aisles and along the perimeter. Further, I was told that fifty people or so responded during each altar call during the height of the revival. From the various people who gave me figures, I got the impression that they, too, wanted to not overshoot the actual numbers. So could there have been 2000 or more people per service? Could the altar call number have been 75 or higher? We don't know, so I have not used such figures. They are, though, certainly within the realm of feasibility.

Chapter 5

1. John I. Durham, *Exodus*, Word Biblical Commentary (Waco, Texas: Word, 1987), pp. 69-70.

Chapter 6

1. Jim Cymbala, *Fresh Wind, Fresh Fire*. Grand Rapids, Michigan: Zondervan Publishing House, 1997.
2. Donald S. Whitney, *Spiritual Disciplines of the Christian Life.* Colorado Springs, Colorado: Navpress Publishing Group, 1991.
3. Jonathan Edwards, 1734, *A Faithful Narrative of the Surpris-*

ing Work of God, Part 1, https://www.cbn.com/spirituallife/
churchandministry/churchhistory/Jonathan_Edwards1.aspx

Epilogue

1. Additionally, there were things I heard that I intentionally
chose to leave out. For me, they weren't as important for
my purpose. I wrote this book to help strengthen the overall
Church in America. If certain details seemed less pertinent
toward achieving that goal, I omitted them.

About the Author

Tom Kraeuter (pronounced Kroyter) is a Bible teacher, author and worship leader. He serves as Executive Director of Training Resources, a ministry devoted to strengthening Christians in their relationships with God and with one another. Tom has ministered in hundreds of churches to tens of thousands of Christians. Tom's ministry is marked by his ability to apply Scripture to everyday situations.

Churches of all sizes have hosted Tom as a special guest and conference speaker. His most popular teachings are on worship and church unity. He has been welcomed by churches in nearly every state, from more than 40 denominations, including Baptist, Evangelical Free, Pentecostal, Lutheran, Presbyterian, Mennonite and Vineyard.

Tom has attended Christian Outreach Church near St. Louis, Missouri, for more than thirty years. He and his wife Barbara have three children.

Contact Tom Kraeuter:

Training Resources, Inc.
65 Shepherds Way
Hillsboro MO 63050
636-789-4522
staff@training-resources.org

Check out our ministry websites

Training-Resources.org

WorshipSeminar.com

WorshipMinute.com

WorshipLeadingAnswers.com

WorshipMinistryDevotions.com

WorshipLeadingCoach.com

WorshipConferenceList.com

WorshipLeaderSummit.com

Other books by Tom Kraeuter

Worship in Heaven... and Why on Earth It Matters

Are There Terrorists in Your Church?

Worshiping God in the Hard Times

Reflecting God's Mercy in an Unmerciful World

Keys to Becoming an Effective Worship Leader

Oh, Grow Up!

Becoming a True Worshiper

The Worship Leader's Handbook

If Standing Together Is So Great,
Why Do We Keep Falling Apart?

Developing an Effective Worship Ministry

Times of Refreshing

Things They Didn't Teach Me in Worship Leading School

The Blessing of Obed-edom

Guiding Your Church Through a Worship Transition

Living Beyond the Ordinary

The Missing Element of Worship

More Things They Didn't Teach Me in Worship Leading School